SAINT JOHN GHOSTS

Conan

Twenty Tales of Strange Happenings in Canada's Third Foggiest City

Dec 14 2015

Enjoy!

DAVID GOSS

Published by
Blue Rock Books
A Division of Words, Walks, Workshops
21 Glenwood Drive
Saint John, N.B. E2M 5P3

Design & Layout by
Corey Dickinson Design
Rothesay, N.B.

Printed by
Taylor Printing Group Inc.
Fredericton, N.B.

Library and Archives Canada Cataloguing in Publication

Goss, David, author
Saint John ghosts : twenty tales of strange happenings in Canada's third foggiest city / by David Goss.

ISBN 978-0-9938660-0-5 (pbk.)

1. Ghosts--New Brunswick--Saint John. 2. Haunted places--New Brunswick--Saint John. I. Title.

BF1472.C3G68 2014 133.109715'32 C2014-905185-9

CONTENTS

Chapter 1 The Ghost of Lady La Tour-The Most Enduring of Saint John's Ghost Tales 7

Chapter 2 The Ghost of West Saint John 13

Chapter 3 The Potato Shed Ghost 19

Chapter 4 Seen in the Mist at Mispec 25

Chapter 5 Two Strange Stories from Saint John East 31

Chapter 6 Loch Lomond Cottage County had its Scary Side 37

Chapter 7 Imelada and the Ghosts of Golden Grove 43

Chapter 8 The Lower Cove Specter 49

Chapter 9 Strange Occurrences at the Venerable Imperial Theatre that are not Readily Explainable 53

Chapter 10 North End Ghosts 59

Chapter 11 Burial Ground Incidents that Affected the Public 67

Chapter 12 Haunted Places of Business 73

Chapter 13 Meet Some Believers 79

Chapter 14 Hauntings on the West Side of Saint John 85

Chapter 15 Centracare had its Share of Ghosts 93

Chapter 16 The Ghost of Black Charlie's Hill in Milford 99

Chapter 17 George Henry Wheaton and the Ghost of Acamac 105

Chapter 18 River Valley Railroad Ghost 111

Chapter 19 Ghosts and the Union Club 117

Chapter 20 Where Do Ghosts Go When They Go? 121

This book is dedicated to my lifelong friend
and fellow West Sider Foster Hammond

In 1995, Foster proposed I share ghost stories at the New River Provincial Park, where he was the manager and that I do it as the ghost of John Roix, who lost his life in the tragic sinking of the ship Genii off New River Island when the Saxby Gale struck the area on October 4, 1869. Foster related that he'd heard many stories in his time at the park of how this ghost had been spotted in countless locations around New River. He encouraged me to talk to local folks like Jackie Oland, Lloyd and Gracie Mealey, Georgie and Charlie Mealey, Shirley Chesley, David and Murial Haggerty to name a few, to see what I could find out. There were plenty of stories to work with, and this piqued my interest in collecting ghost stories of that area, and other areas of New Brunswick, including, of course, Saint John, which this book covers.

Enjoy these stories, and share them as you gather around the campfire in summer, or huddle by the fireplace on cold winter nights. If a story comes up that you would like to share, I'd love to hear it so be sure to contact me at gosswalk@nbnet.nb.ca or by mail at 21 Glenwood Drive, Saint John, E2M 5P3 or speak to me on one of the summer Tuesday night Walk n' Talks, where Saint John's past comes to life in folklore and factual happenings and occasionally in a ghost tale or two.

David Goss
July 23, 2014

Something to
think about as you
read these stories:

"Though a great deal is too strange to be believed, nothing is too strange to have happened."

English novelist
Thomas Hardy
1840-1928

David Goss as the Ghost of John on the left and the man who first suggested the role that piqued his interest in ghost tales; Foster Hammond, is to the right.

Introduction by Diana Grant,
founder of the Loyalist City Paranormal Group

The paranormal has intrigued me for as long as I can remember. Having lived in Saint John for years and in buildings where I've had strange occurrences, I felt strongly that the city was steeped in the unknown, the unexplained and the unseen. My need to know more about the city's local lore and legends intensified, leading me to story teller David Goss. David shared with me the story of Maggie Vail, a young woman murdered in 1868 in the prime of her life along with her infant daughter. He also told of Daniel Keymore the fisherman that drowned off the Shag Rock in Bay of Fundy at the mouth of Saint John Harbour, the sightings of Lady Latour's ghost at Fort La Tour and across the harbour on the streets of Carleton, and so many more local stories. David has also shared with me the many supposedly haunted locations that he knew of in Saint John, some of which I've even had the opportunity to investigate for the presence of paranormal activity.

With sightings of the recently or long since departed having occurred as far back as has been recorded, one cannot help but wonder what lies in store for us once our bodies cease to work. Is there something more for us on this earth? Are we able to come back and visit or are we doomed to spend eternity wandering where we once lived? A belief in the paranormal or the other side is not required for a person to be passionate about the subject. It's the thought of what could be or the possibility of such things that keeps us wondering about and in my case seeking the unexplained.

This collection of stories will give you something to think about as you travel about the Saint John area. Not a section of the city is missed…and these, David tells me, are only a few of the stories that have been shared with him. I hope you enjoy them as much as I did.

Chapter 1

The Ghost of Lady La Tour

The Most Enduring of Saint John's Ghost Tales

The Ghost of Lady La Tour– the Most Enduring of Saint John's Ghost Tales

Reports of the sighting of the ghost of Marie de La Tour are the most enduring of all Saint John ghost tales. Reports of her appearance have occurred on both sides of the harbour since her death defending her husband's fort at the mouth of the St. John River in 1645.

The story is not as well known as it might be, for it is not often shared with schoolchildren as part of the curriculum. Thus, students are usually very surprised to learn of her exploits when I take groups to the site of Fort La Tour on the Harbour Passage on a bluff just below the Lord Beaverbrook Rink. There they are fascinated to see the figures of the principals of the story through Albert Deveau's chain-saw-woodcarving of the La Tour's and their mortal enemy Charles D'Aulnay.

To understand the story that follows, it is necessary to know the La Tour story, so what follows is a brief account of the couple's life in Saint John.

Both Charles La Tour and Charles D'Aulnay believed they had rights to the fur trade at the mouth of the River St. John, but it was La Tour who established a fort there and eventually brought his wife Francoise Marie Jacqueline from the big city of Paris to the wilderness of North America.

When she arrived in 1640, he proudly showed her the fort he had rebuilt overlooking the harbour. It was considered the prime location in all of what was to become the Maritimes for conducting fur trading with the natives. Almost from the day Marie arrived, there were constant skirmishes with D'Aulnay and his forces, and eventually, Marie Jacqueline returned to France to appeal for help. She stayed for eight months, and then returned to assist her husband in his battles at Fort La Tour. Both Marie Jacqueline and her husband spent time in Boston, where he had engaged in trading, in hopes of getting support in their fight against D'Aulnay. It was while La Tour was on his own in Massachusetts in the spring of 1645 that D'Aulnay raided Fort La Tour once again. On that occasion he was let into the fort by a Swiss traitor, thus captured the fortress and proceeded to hang all within, save the traitor and one other man who agreed to do the hangings. Francoise, her son and one other woman were also spared. As lead defender of her husband's fort, Marie was made to watch as one by one her men were hung. On April 16, 1645, Easter Sunday, she died, it is said of a broken heart. The next day, she was buried behind the fort. D'Aulney then had the prime fortress location is what was called Acadia, but in time, when D'Aulney died, and La Tour married his widow, he once again took it over.

Many years passed between 1645 and the arrival of New England colonists in 1763 and during that time there is no record of any happenings in what was to become Saint John.

To my knowledge, the early Simonds, Hazen and White records do not report any ghostly accounts, despite the fact they settled on land that was the former location of the fort and its surrounding graveyard. The earliest written account that shows up that purports to be of Lady La Tour describes her as a "lady in the style of 200 years ago" and is found in the Ganong Scrapbooks # 4 page 26 and is an account of the ghost of Lady La Tour, which describes her as being a "little woman with silver gray hair wandering strangely about, flitting here and there in the night like a will o' wisp, peering anxiously out toward the harbour one minute as if awaiting somebody's return, and then walking back among the modern houses to shed a few more tears."

Ganong's clipping identifies the storyteller as Navy Island fisherman Jack Sinclair and he is recounting what he and other "west end people," had seen.

In the year 1883, a more detailed account of Sinclair's sightings of Lady La Tour appears in the Saint John Sun. It says he is living on Navy Island, as did Ganong's account. That Island was about a third of the way across the channel between the western side of Saint John Harbour and Long

Wharf on the north side. It was just offshore of what was then thought to be Fort La Tour, but which, upon investigation later, turned out to be Fort Frederick. Sinclair had invited a reporter to come to his home and regaled him with tales of meeting Lady La Tour on the island and in the streets of Saint John West. At the time, Sinclair was living with his mother and father, who he claimed had seen the ghost many times, and it seems likely that Jack Sinclair in Ganong's account was the father of this boy. On the day of the interview, August 11, 1883 the younger Sinclair claimed to have seen the ghost only four days earlier walking along the island's beach when he had come back to the island from Carleton, the old name for Saint John West. He described the ghost as "attired in a silk, gray dress and wore white stockings with black stripes. She wore no bonnet. Her dress was very long, having a train of considerable length. The sleeves of the dress were loose and quite short."

Now even the most doubtful would have to admit that Jimmy saw something! How many men could give such a full description of a woman's appearance without having experienced it? It is just not something men typically do very well.

No doubt the reporter came to this conclusion too and thus pressed on with the interview, for which we are grateful, as he managed to collect many more ghostly details. For example, Jimmy asked the ghost to confirm her presence; to confirm she was buried near the old fort; and to confirm that only a few of her bones remained in the ground. He told the reporter Lady La Tour had answered his questions in the affirmative. Then he asked the ghost if any jewels or money were buried with her, and her answer was in the negative.

However, he said, Lady La Tour had revealed to him the location of gold buried in Carleton; at Pisarinco, (Lorneville today) and told him there was a million dollars buried in Long Island Sound in New York. "It is my intention to find it," Jimmy told the reporter.

Besides Lady La Tour (incidentally she never used that name during her lifetime, for as was the custom of the time, she retained her maiden name though married,) the Sinclair family claimed to have seen the brother of D'Aulnay Charnissay on one occasion and an unknown woman who passed through the walls of their home when they approached her on another. They also reported having seen a soldier with his lady friend walking across the island on another occasion and on another, a red-coated British soldier complete with epaulettes wandering about with his throat cut from ear to ear.

The fact that the actual site of Fort La Tour was not on the west side at all was unknown to the Sinclair's and to everyone else in Saint John until the mid 1950's. That's when extensive excavations of the Portland Point, on the harbour front across the water from Navy Island, made it clear from the levels in which artifacts were found that it had been, firstly, a popular site for the Aboriginal people as far back as 2000 BC, and later had had two forts built on it some 400 years ago, (the La Tours) and 250 years ago, was the site of a trading post and shipbuilding building activity (Simonds, Hazen and White).

The factual information contained in this story is verifiable and can be augmented on reading the very excellent 1983 book "Fortune and La Tour," by M. A. Macdonald. A highly readable, yet scholarly tome, she did not delve into the folklore of the La Tours, and there is no mention of ghosts in her book. She does say, however, that the graves of Lady La Tour and her men have not been found.

This however, has not prevented locals that lived in the area from claiming that they know exactly where the graves are and that they have chased Lady La Tour from their homes and watched her disappear into the fog. I could not begin to tell of the number of people who have shared such a story with me. I think the most vivid account was given by a family who lived at Portland Point before Urban Renewal in the 1960's. They said they had regular problems with material they wished to store neatly in their basement being tossed about at night. For weeks all would be quiet, and their carefully shelved seasonal clothing, their barrels of flour, sugar, and molasses would be fine, then one night, they would hear a commotion downstairs and, when they checked in the morning, the contents of the basement would lie strewn about the floor. Barrels of flour would be overturned, sugar spilled across the floor, molasses left to drain from spigots.

It was suggested to them that perhaps their house had been built on the graves of Lady La Tour and her men, but they dismissed the idea. However, in doing some renovations to the basement walls made of quarried limestone from nearby Fort Howe, they discovered a doorway that had been boarded over. When they opened the door they found there was a tunnel which lead toward the harbour. Based on its position, it occurred to them that it might pass right under Fort La Tour. To do so, it had to pass by the gravesite of the famed Lady, or so they concluded. So, with local stone from Fort Howe, the same stone that had been used to build the foundation in the era of Simonds, Hazen and White, they sealed the tunnel, and had no further problems with disruption in the basement.

A coincidence? Perhaps, but the story of the ghost of Lady La Tour endures and from time to time to this day, a call comes to this writer that someone has spotted something they don't understand in the mists of Portland Point, or along the foggy waterfront in Saint John West, and the old belief that it might be the ghost of Saint John's first heroine comes to the fore once more.

Navy Island was home to many fishermen in 1883 when Jimmy Sinclair shared his stories about Lady La Tour. In this photo, the last of the residents are being moved off the island in 1932. At that time, it was still believed Fort La Tour was on the west side of the harbour, and though this was later proved incorrect, the stories of the ghost of Lady La Tour continued to be told on the West Side until recent times.

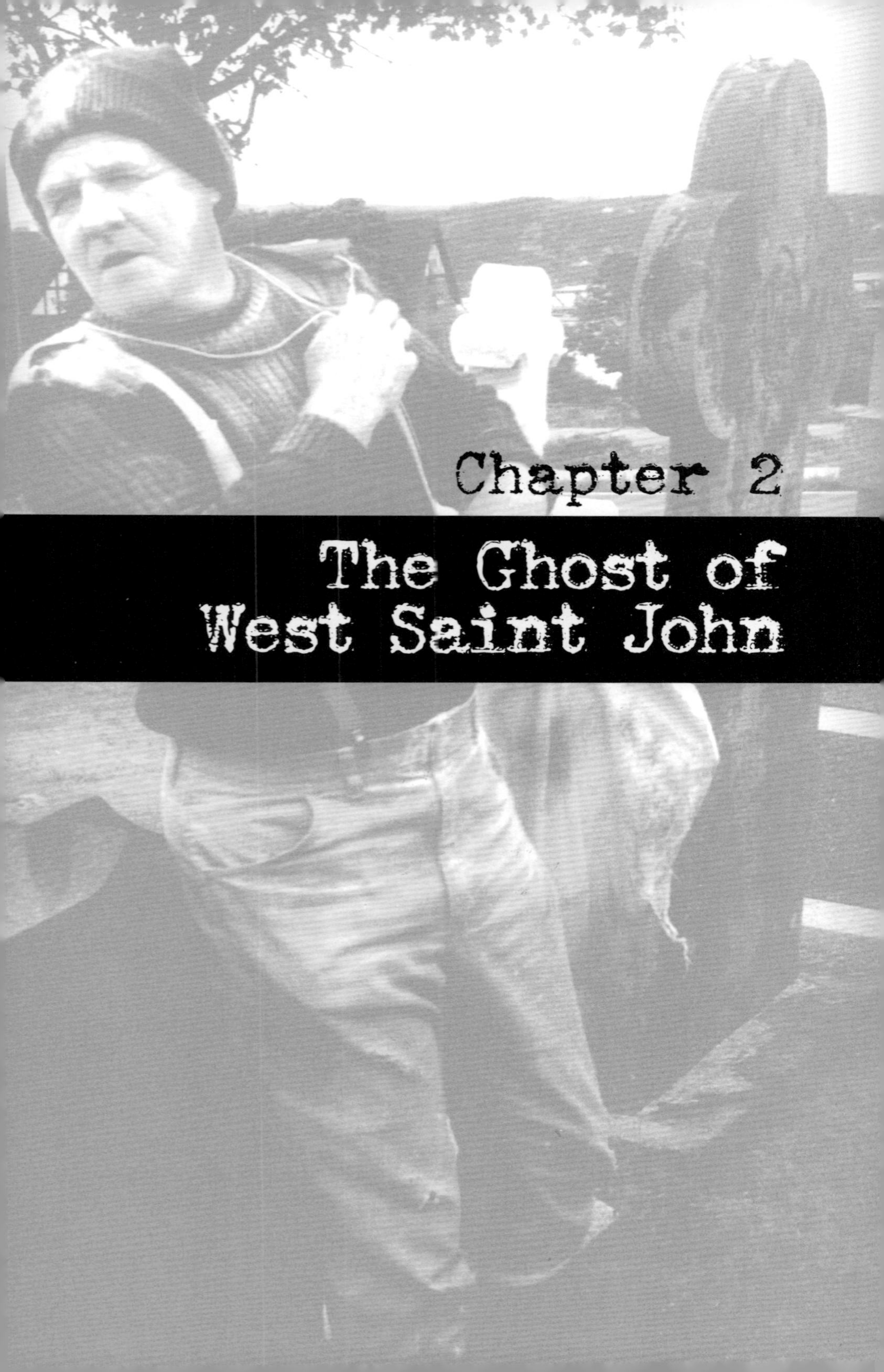

Chapter 2

The Ghost of West Saint John

The Ghost of West Saint John

The second best known Saint John ghost story is also centered around the harbour, and the same Navy Island area as the La Tour story. This story has been told and retold for decades, and I first learned of the Ghost of Daniel Keymore in a "Man on the Street" column in the Evening Times Globe of July 17, 1975. The author of these daily pieces of local trivia were never identified, but the editors depended on Saint Johners who had stories to share to call them with their tales, thus, many unusual items that would have remained unknown as they were usually shared orally, can be, fortunately, found in the columns. While the person who retold the story is unknown, a long time west sider, Murray Burley, shared a version of it with me the late 90's as a tale that was one that his salmon fisherman dad had shared with he and his siblings when he was growing up in Carleton in the 30's. The story itself dates back at least to the 1880's, when Sinclair shared his La Tour story with the media.

It is, without doubt, the most often printed story of ghostly happenings in Saint John. Nationally, John Robert Columbo did the story and called it The Codfish Man and New Brunswick author Stuart Trueman did it in his book "Tall Tales and True Tales from Down East." In fact, as Trueman often wrote the "Man on the Street" column, and was the long time editor of the Evening Times Globe, he may have been the man behind the 1975 story. Regionally, Nova Scotians Steve Vernon did the story in Wicked Woods; Reg Jessom did it in on television and in his book Maritime Mysteries and Vernon Oickle covered it in his book, Ghost Stories of the Maritimes.

I suspect it will endure as all these writers did the story in their own way, thus adding to the Keymore legend.

What follows is my version of the tale which I have shared since 1978 on Walks n' Talks in the area of Saint John where Keymore lived, died, and where his ghost was often seen.

"When the fishermen of Carleton – now called Saint John West, -saw gulls flying over the tidal rips of Hilyard's Reef across from their riverside fishing sheds on Navy Island,(where the toll plaza on the bridge stood) they knew the annual spring run of gaspereau were making their way upriver. Soon their nets would be heavy with fresh spring fish.

Among those leaving their Carleton homes at dawn on the morning of April 18, 1889 was Daniel Keymore. Before he left, his wife asked if he had heard the news that the city was to build a bridge across the harbour, and that it was to be supported by the land of Navy Island where Keymore's fishing gear was kept and from which the Carleton fishermen departed each day on their quest for fish. Daniel told his wife that if the city ever took the island for that purpose, he would haunt them eternally. Of course, it was just in jest, but as it turned out, it was no idle threat.

On that morning long ago Keymore launched his dory from Navy Island, lifted the sail, and caught the wind. He soon passed the wharves of Carleton, the mid harbour Rodney floats and the harbour ferry dock, then in the outer harbour the Beacon Light, and finally, went sailing past the light and famed foghorn of Partridge Island, around which most of the men fished.

That day Keymore decided to travel further out into the bay westward to the Shag Rocks. Still, from his position about half way to Manawagonish Island, he could see his home on the bluff behind Bay Shore where his wife often came out and waved to him as he fished. But his peaceful day was soon to change as a storm suddenly blew up and Keymore's boat was swamped. He was drowned in the cold water of the Bay of Fundy within sight of his house.

The other fishermen returned to Carleton safely but Keymore's wife and children waited in vain for his return. On the morning after his drowning, his wife went out to the porch of their home and looked up and down the Bay Shore. She was hoping against hope to see her husband, by some miracle, appear. Instead, she found only a huge cod fish on her doorstep. Keymore never showed up nor was his body ever found.

One year later, on the anniversary of Keymore's death, his widow stepped out on the doorway and onto her porch to scan the bay as she had done every day since Daniel had disappeared. On that day she found a huge cod fish on the porch of her home and for the next six years, on April 18th, a cod fish mysteriously appeared on the doorstep. On the seventh year, Mrs. Keymore had remarried and moved her family to a new home down in Carleton about one mile away. That year on the anniversary of Keymore's death, the house he and his wife had shared mysteriously burned to the ground. The firemen who responded to the flames found only a pile of ashes with a huge cod fish on the top.

Over those seven years many residents of Carleton reported to have seen a phantom figure leaving the Navy Island area, and noted that he carried a huge codfish as he walked through the community on the morning of April 18th. Though many tried to follow him, they always lost him as he took a circuitous route through Carleton in the early morning mist. However, it was generally believed he was the one leaving the cod fish at the Keymore home and that when his wife abandoned that home; he burned it, and left as a sign, the huge codfish.

After that, the ghost no longer roamed," and that is the way most of those who recount the story end it.

However, I chose to continue the story and bring it up to the present day. So, this is what I say.

"In 1968, the city finally kept the 1889 promise to open a bridge from uptown to Carleton. Everyone was happy to see the new link completed and looking forward to it one day being attached to a modern highway leading east and west, and making travel around the city and the outskirts much easier.

At least that was the case among the living. Among the dead, however, there was one man who was not happy, one man who had told his wife long ago that if the city took his fishing shack and impeded his opportunity to fish, he would be back to haunt the area.

It seems he kept that promise, for on the morning of April 18, 1969, drivers coming to the toll plaza at the Harbour Bridge were startled to see a ragged old fisherman carrying a huge codfish on his back cross the ten lanes of traffic as if there was not a car moving. In fact, there soon wasn't a car in motion, for no one wanted to hit the ragged old fellow, and drivers stopped in their tracks, honked their horns, rolled down their windows and shouted words that can't be repeated in polite company. The wispy ragged figure just ambled on as if nothing were going on. Once he got to the King Street side of the toll plaza, he ambled up King, and later, reports said he was seen on Prince Street, then near Martello Tower, and finally crossing the rail line on Sea Street and down to the location of the old Keymore homestead.

Those who knew the story, which had been kept alive by the fishermen and longshoremen of the West Side, said emphatically, 'It's Daniel Keymore, he said he'd come back to haunt the area if a bridge was built, and he's done it.'

Daniel's appearance only happened on April 18th, the anniversary of his death, but it was dramatic enough that the Harbour Bridge people did not want to see the event repeated. After all, they were having enough trouble getting folks to use the only toll bridge in the province, and, a bridge that, at the time, didn't do much but get people from the north end and uptown to the West Side as the throughway was still being built.

So, the Harbour Bridge Authority contacted the professors at the University of New Brunswick in Saint John, (UNBSJ), which was just new to the city at that time, and asked them to study the matter. UNBSJ sent some students over to the toll plaza area where the disturbing apparition had been seen to asses the situation. After due deliberation, they came up with a plausible explanation for the ghostly figure that many claimed had crossed the throughway. Nearby was a 201 foot grain elevator. In fact, it practically loomed over the toll plaza. It was a massive hulk of a building between the rising sun, and the plaza. 'What people are seeing,' the UNBSJ students concluded, 'is that when the sun comes up, it hits that grain elevator, and creates a shadow in the plaza area. There's no ghost, just a shadowy patch of darkness that moves across the plaza.'

Well, the Harbour Bridge authorities were relieved, and some people believed the explanation they passed along to the public, as it was coming from the professors and the learned students they were teaching. But others remained sceptical...and with good reason it seems. In 1994 that grain elevator was torn down, and to this day, some of those driving into the sun rise on the early morning of April 18 report they see a shadowy figure carrying a cod fish and walking across the busy traffic lanes where harbour bridge toll plaza once stood.'

Then I would invite people to check on this story themselves the next time April 18 came up on the calendar. I don't know if anyone ever did, but I do know it got them thinking that just maybe there was something behind this enduring story of Daniel Keymore.

The story of the ghost of Daniel Keymore has been kept alive by David Goss, appearing here in Cedar Hill cemetery, which Daniel passed through when carrying his codfish on his way to his Bay shore area home overlooking the rocks where he drowned. Photo by Harold Wright.

Chapter 3

The Potato Shed Ghost

The Potato Shed Ghost

While we're in the vicinity of the harbour, let's have one more story that has a connection with the waterfront. When I was looking for information about a ghost said to haunt Saint John's Martello Tower I visited octogenarian Basil Hamilton at his City Line home, as I had heard he served as a guard in the tower during the Second World War. He confirmed that he indeed spent many a long and lonely night on guard in the tower in the 40's but added emphatically, "I don't think there are any ghosts in Martello Tower, and I am sure if there were, I would have seen them, I would have heard them, I would have felt them."

"But Basil," I protested, "I've been told they were there....that folks living near Seaside Park who had to go to the West side were afraid to pass the Tower at night. That they would hear moaning from the dungeon and chains would rattle."

"Well," he said, "I heard no such thing in my time there."

"Tell me about that?" I replied.

He filled me in, saying, "During the Second World War I was among the first to be stationed there. We were placed there on shifts at night to watch for German submarines and enemy boats coming into the harbour. At the time there were no outside contacts-no telephones connecting anyone. It was mighty lonely work. There were just two of us in the Tower. We went from top to bottom checking things out. I'm certain that if there was anything strange in that Tower, we would have encountered it."

"Well Basil," I said, "I suppose you'd say that there is no ghost of West Saint John either?"

By that, I was referring to the story you have already read about Daniel Keymore.

"Oh, I know there is a ghost in West Saint John. I know that story. I've heard it time and again," he said.

"Well, tell me the story," I said. I expected a version of the tale of Daniel Keymore who, you'll recall, carries the cod fish up Prince Street to his old home near the Tower on the anniversary of his death each April 18th. I was in for a surprise. Basil told me of a new ghost of West Saint John which he called the "Potato Shed Ghost." This is his tale:

"There was a fisherman in the harbour in the 1880's. He was out off the Shag Rocks working his nets when he noticed a strange boat moving in toward Sheldon's Point. He was curious, and decided to drift by and see what was going on. As he watched, he noticed they were unloading bags and storing them in a cave at the end of the point. He let the boat drift a bit closer hoping to see what it was they were stashing. He thought they would think he was fishing if they spotted him. Eventually they came out of the cave and spotted him, and he could tell from their faces they were not happy to have been seen. In fact, they gave chase. The fisherman raised the sail on his little sloop and skidded across the waves as fast as he could toward the West Side. He thought he'd lose them around the Beacon Light, but they kept following right in to the shore, and past the weirs at Beatteay's Beach. So he beached his boat by the beach bathing dock, and took off running toward the rail tracks, hoping to meet up with some of the workers on a railway section crew, or lose his pursuers among the tenements of Protection Street. But he wasn't fast enough and they caught up with him at the edge of the Blue Rock, and there they beat him to death. They buried his body under some debris, and left the scene.

The fisherman was missed right away, but as his boat was found on the shore it was thought the boat must have drifted in and its owner must have drowned fishing off the Shag Rocks. Such incidents happened frequently enough back then so when a body did not show up, the fisherman was soon forgotten as just one more harbour drowning.

Then around the turn of the 20th century when the grain elevator and the wharves were being developed in West Saint John bones were found when the foundations were being dug, but no one could identify the remains. So piers twelve, thirteen, and fourteen were constructed right on top of the rocks not far from where the bones had been discovered. Pier fourteen became known as the 'Potato Shed' as it was where most of the potatoes were shipped out of the harbour. The longshoremen and truckers who worked in there would often tell of the ghost of the potato shed. They'd be lifting the heavy bags onto pallets and would see a wisp of something running between the sacks as if trying to get a look at what they were doing. This, of course, is just as the fisherman had been doing when the men at Sheldon's Point saw him, chased him, and then murdered him.

Some of the truckers and longshoremen got so spooked being watched by the constantly shifting figure among the stacks of potato sacks that they refused to work the potato shed at all.

That shed is gone now. The ghost may have found somewhere else to do its haunting, but one thing I'm sure of Dave is that it isn't Martello Tower," Basil said with conviction as he ended his story of the Ghost of West Saint John, which I prefer to call the story of the "Potato Shed Ghost."

When Basil Hamilton worked as a guard at Martello Tower during World War Two, the concrete observation area was added to the 1812-1815 defense tower, changing its looks dramatically, but according to him, it gave ghosts no more places to hide as there aren't any ghosts there. However, he knew of another ghost in the area which he shared in this story of the "Potato Shed Ghost."

This is a rare image of Beatty's Beach, as it was spelled on what appears to have been a postcard image about 1914. The beach with the boats, raft for working weirs, and diving pier was where the unfortunate observer in Hamilton's story met his end.

Walks n' Talks, such as this one at Martello Tower, have been a good way to share ghost tales, but, as you have learned, Martello does not seem to have a ghost.

Chapter 4

Seen in the Mist at Mispec

Seen in the Mist at Mispec

While we're still on the water of the Bay of Fundy for this story, we've moved east of the city about 10 kilometers to a very rural area known as Mispec, where Mispec Park is found.

Mispec Beach has been a popular ocean side experience with Saint Johners for more than a century, being a beach that visitors loved to visit even though it had no official status as a public beach. Though it is just outside the city limits, it came under city control after World War Two, as part of the war assets dispersal around Saint John.

Many consider it Saint John's best beach for sunbathing because of the amphitheatre style of layout of the long stretch of soft sand between the very cold Bay of Fundy and the embankment on which the city established a canteen, washrooms, and built a well equipped playground.

In recent years, many improvements were made to the beach by a citizens group and these included the addition of walking trails, a new ball field and a couple of additional stairway accesses to the beach itself. However, a storm in the winter of 2011 did severe damage to the area, and though it appeared the city would abandon it as one of their recreational sites, when Canaport stepped in to offer help, the city changed it position and the beach is open again.

Mispec Beach can be packed on sunny days, but on foggy days the beach is often deserted, and even the several kilometers of well laid out trails behind the beach do not draw visitors.

Thus, the beach can become a spooky spot on foggy days so it is just as well that there are no visitors at such times, for this is when the ghost of Mispec Beach often chooses to wander.

The ghost has been written about since December 1873, when treasure was found in the forest behind the beach. It was quite a nice treasure, too, being a box that was three feet long, fourteen inches wide and twelve inches deep that was filled with silver and gold coins.

The treasure was soon dispersed among those who found it, and those who heard about it and came to buy a souvenir portion of what they called "Captain Kidd's" treasure. Many scoffed at the story, but dozens flocked to the area to seek some of the treasure as one of the rumours that circulated at the time was that there was lots of booty remaining to be found.

However, not everyone was anxious to come to Mispec, for along with stories of the possibilities of treasure was the equally told tale of the ghost of a headless man that guarded the treasure of Mispec. Beryl Rutherford shared this story with me on a visit on July 08, 2004.

"We have a place here we call Ghost Hollow. My grandfather Ring lived there, just this side, (the Mispec Beach side) of the bridge. I heard him say that there was a chest of gold buried in the hill and that there were a bunch of people that came to dig it up. They dug and dug, and they came to the chest, but they could not get it out of the ground. It just would not budge. So they got a team of oxen, and a chain was fastened to the chest, and the oxen were told to 'git up.' They tried very hard to pull that chest out of the ground, and they were actually making some headway, with the chest about half way out, and then all of a sudden, the oxen were just hauled backwards. They could not get a hold on the ground and they were just sucked into the hole and disappeared. It just covered over (with earth) as if no one had ever dug it out. Now, the reason they call the area Ghost Hollow, is that one of the men who was working there lost his head when the oxen were being pulled into the hole. One of the horns just cut his head right off as it went by. Since then, late at night, and sometimes on very foggy days, he's seen walking the road from the bridge to Mispec Beach, and carrying his head in a bag. People meet him on the road and they say 'hello' but he never says a word."

At the time of the telling of the story, Beryl's sister, Thelma, was present.

She added information about the headless man, saying, "When people walk that road, they will hear footsteps behind them, but when they turn, there is never anyone there. If they speed up, the footsteps behind them will speed up."

On the night of August 8, 2004, I shared this story with participants in a ghost walk at Mispec Park. That night, when participants left the park, they encountered a rough looking ghost walking the road, his head in his hand. Though it was a set up, (Harold Wright and his daughter Jessalyn were the ghosts), I was later told two boys from England were with the group, and they were so convinced they had seen the Mispec ghost, they could not sleep that night. Now, of course, the ghost tale is international, for no doubt those boys shared it once back home. Fair exchange, I'd say, as more than a few of our ghost stories, perhaps even this one, are based on British tales, as some believe it to be the most haunted nation in the world.

Mispec Beach is an inviting place to spend a sunny day, but on foggy days and moonless nights, it can be a different story if the headless ghost wanders in the park.

Where the Mispec River drains into the Bay of Fundy is where the headless ghost of Mispec is most often seen on foggy days and moonless nights.

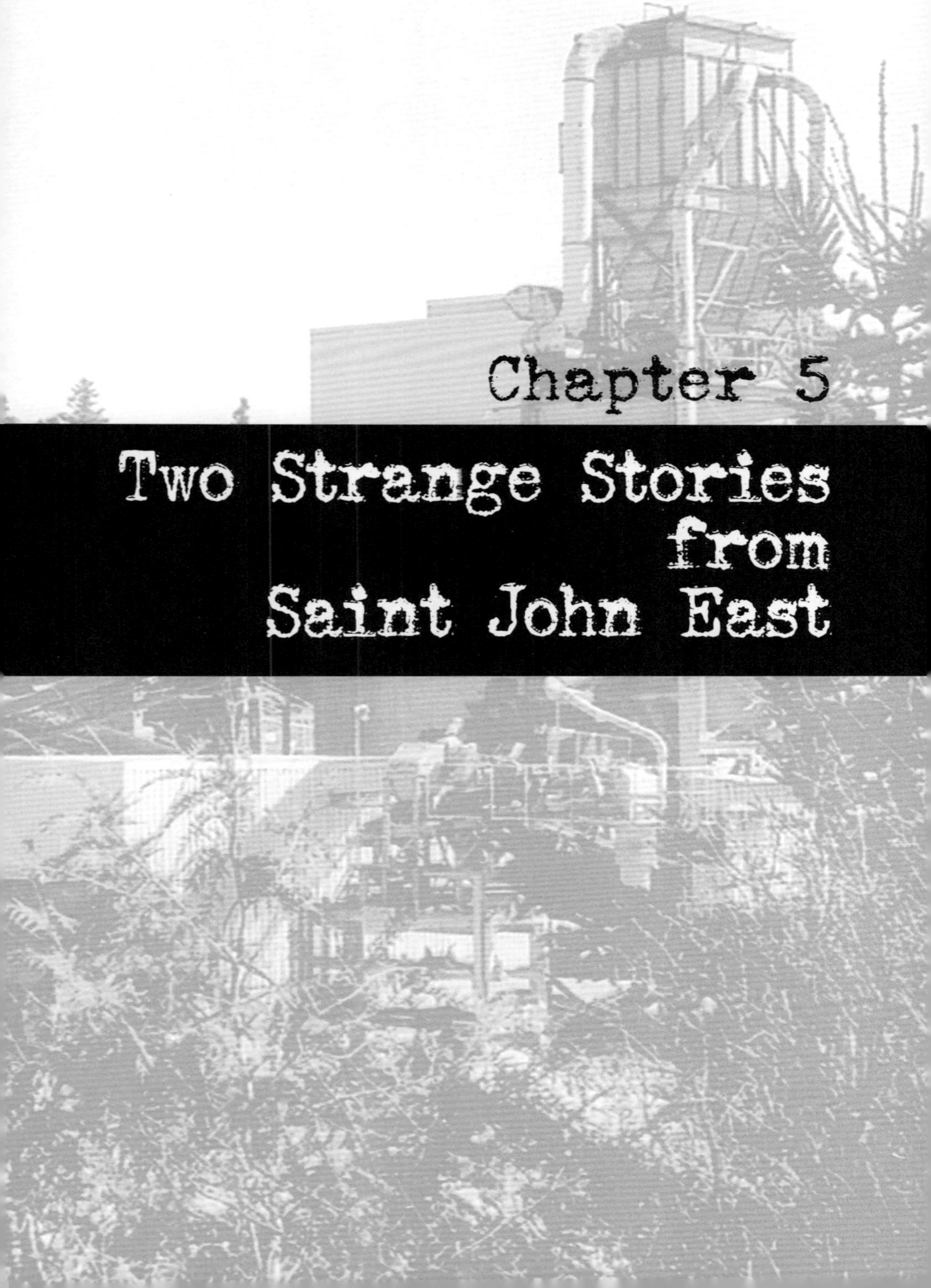

Chapter 5

Two Strange Stories from Saint John East

Two Strange Stories from Saint John East

The next three chapters will keep us in the east of the city. I am doing this on purpose, as over the four decades I have offered Walks n' Talks, written columns and done books, I have been accused of favouring the west of the city. Some say my motto is "West is best." Well, I am guilty as charged, but only because being a west sider, I grew up with stories from that area, and know more people in that area, and I have found, with collecting stories, that if you are a known commodity, people are more likely to share with you. So, I don't believe there is a bias on my part, simply proximity to people with tales to tell.

As you will see in the following pages, all good stories are not west side stories. Here are two I collected that are among many that have come from the east of the city and are well worth sharing.

When you hear tales like those that follow, you are left wondering how many more there are out there that will never be recorded.

Both of these stories may well have been lost if the tellers had not cared to share them with someone who would listen and record what they had to say.

John Watson and Teegan Scott are the two storytellers. Let's defer to age and share John's tale first. I begin by noting that lime quarrying and burning was the first industry engaged in by Simonds, Hazen and White upon their arrival in Saint John in 1763, and believe it or not, the quarrying is still going on to this day. One of the major quarrying operators is the Brookville Lime Company in an extensive limestone ridge just east of the throughway interchange with Rothesay Avenue. It's actually part of the first grant to Simonds himself, which, of course, has been greatly chopped up in two hundred and twenty five plus years of building Saint John.

John, who is a very dignified descendent of those first Loyalists, and has served as an officer with the Loyalist Society is not one who you would expect to share ghostly tales. Tales of the adventures of the first settlers, their hardships, their romances, their successes, yes, that's what you expect from John, especially when he is all decked out in Loyalist garb, and attending some official function.

It was at just such an occasion, a church parade to historic Trinity Church, often called the "Church of the Loyalists," that John whispered to me, " I hear you're looking for ghost stories...well, I've got one and when we get a minute alone, I'll share it."

And later he did. This is what John said:

"I grew up in Glen Falls, and in 1946 my great uncle, Stan Dixon came to live with the family. He related the story which probably occurred when Stan was an employee of the Brookville Lime works which is near enough to Glen Falls that he could walk from the Watson home to his place of employment. Stan was a bachelor and enjoyed storytelling. One of his most interesting stories was of working at the lime quarry one night and while standing in front of the sheds, one of his fellow employees, white as a ghost and shaking like a leaf, came to the front of the building. Stan asked him what had happened out in the yard. The man replied; 'If you saw what I saw, then you would never go out there!'

'What did you see?' asked Stan. 'I saw a man without a head out wandering around the yard.'

The two men spent the rest of the night working in the shed and stayed out of the yard.

The following morning the fellow got on his bike and went home. He never came back to work at the Brookville Lime operations.

"Stan later learned that there was once a man killed in the works, and he had been decapitated," John said in concluding his story. "Thus, perhaps there is a reason for the ghost of the Brookville Lime works."

Equally, there is a reason why a women's statue in Fernhill Cemetery has only one arm, and though it has a ghostly element, it is not something a ghost did, but a human action that seemed ghostlike.

I have been conducting tours of Fernhill Cemetery for some years now, and in one of the oldest sections there is a marvellous figure of a one armed woman standing some 30 feet off the ground on a fluted column. Carved into the base of the column that holds the statue is the story of the man to whom the work is dedicated, one Walker Tisdale. It reads: "Walker Tisdale, who was born of Loyalist parents after the evacuation of the British on board His Majesty's ship 'Brothers' on passage from New York to this province and departed this life on the 24th day of November 1857, in the 75th year of his age."

This epitaph offers no clue about the identity of the lady on the top of the column. Is it Tisdale's mother, sister, wife? Why does she have only one arm? It had always perplexed me.

So, I was delighted when teen Teegan Scott sidled up to me on a walk one August night and said, "Don't you know how she lost her arm, Mr Goss?"

"Do you?" I asked, with surprise in my voice I'm sure.

"Sure do," she responded. "Our teacher Diane O'Keefe had us out here on a study session, and she told us the story. Seems a long time ago, there was a caretaker's cottage in this area. He kept hearing strange noises at night in the plots around the Tisdale monument. He thought there were spooks loose, so he'd come out with his gun and fire off a few warning shots. One hit the lady and her arm fell off."

Well, it was such a good story, I had Teegan tell the whole crowd. They certainly enjoyed her tale. But I don't think too many believed it.

The next day, I thought I'd check with Fernhill's manager Ann Maloughney about the account, and see if it was widely known. She assured me that Teegan's story was, in fact, a long told tale, and said that the "first caretaker Joshua Clayton is the gentleman who did the shooting." She added, "The story has been passed down over the years, and is often shared with visitors who are interested in the graveyard's history."

It's nice to know that long told tales continue to be shared by a new generation of storytellers, and that from what we can see, that will be the case for some time to come.

Quarrying operations have been going on in Saint John since before the Loyalists arrived, and it is likely ghostly apparitions have been going on for just as long.

The lime burning kilns were a common sight in Saint John a century ago, but as they became obsolete, they took on the moniker, "Silent Sentinels." If they could speak, perhaps they would know what Stan saw at the lime yard in Brookville.

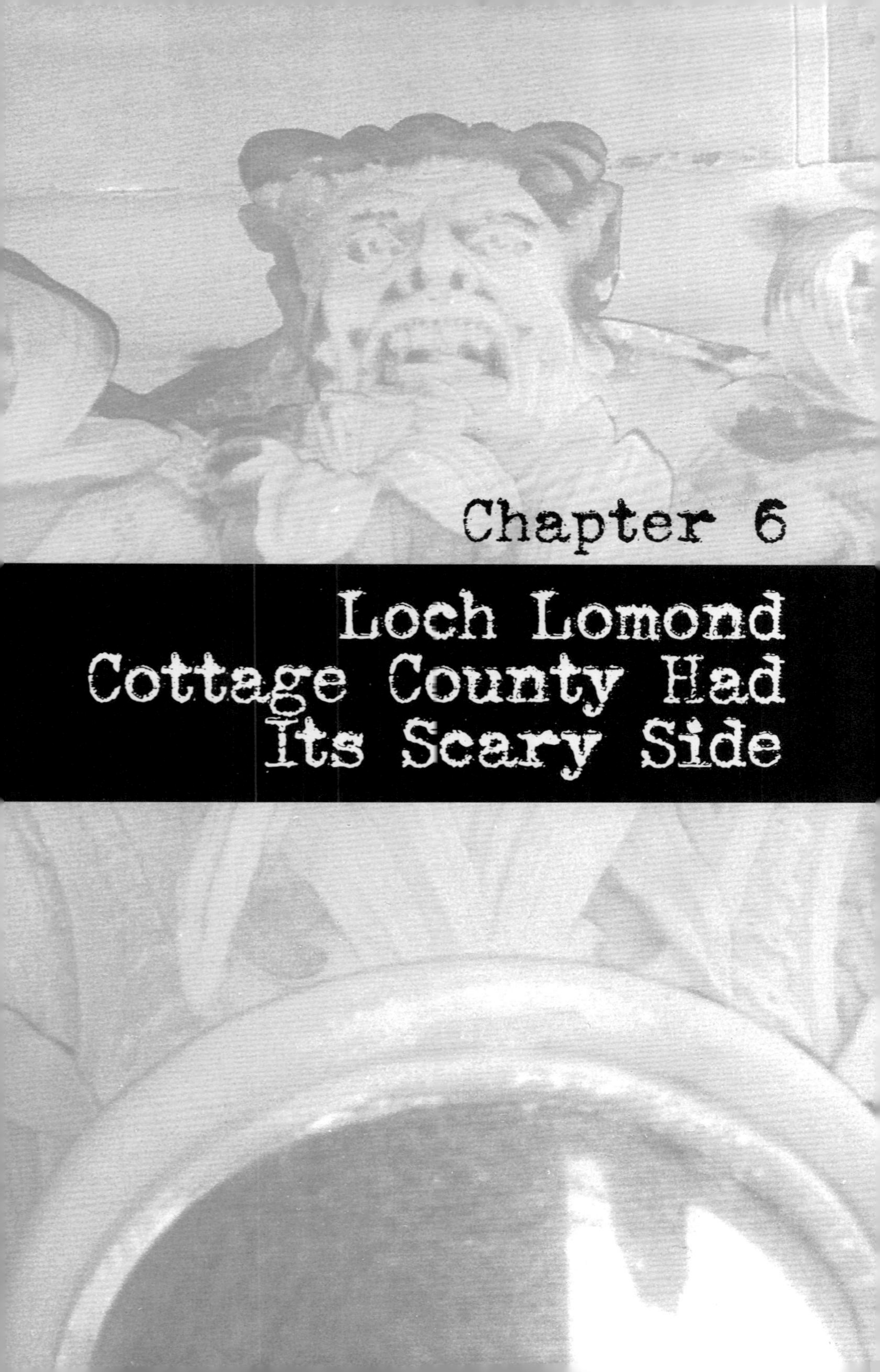

Chapter 6

Loch Lomond Cottage County Had Its Scary Side

Loch Lomond Cottage County Had Its Scary Side

Art Gregg and Greg Walsh look over the 1883 Rogerson Centennial Clock which now resides in the Mayor's Office, City Hall.

Sometimes collecting eerie stories happens in a round about way. That was the situation when I met Greg Walsh who was into his ninth decade when he told me his story of how he had come into the possession of the famed woodcarver John Rogerson's Centennial Clock. This beautiful piece was carved in 1883 to mark the City of Saint John's 100th birthday. Greg called on me because he was wondering what he could do to ensure this treasure lived on after he was gone. Eventually, Greg was able to donate the clock to the City of Saint John and it was hung July 2001 in what was then known as the Red Room, which was and is where guests of the mayor are entertained. Thus, the 1883 Centennial symbol will live on, and the memory of Greg's wife Marie to which the clock is dedicated will live on, too.

It was while working with Greg on this project that he came to trust me, and shared the eerie tales that follow which he had not told anyone since his youth when he summered in the area east of Saint John city known as Loch Lomond.

Greg said, "Till the city bought the lakeside properties to protect them for their watershed, 'or tricked us out of it'." he laughed, "the Loch Lomond Lake area was prime cottage country. Stories of screams in the night, ghosts, and visits from the devil were part of the cottage experience," Greg said in a matter of fact manner.

He went on to say, "The Loch Lomond area was remote 80 years ago, and we had a cottage on Third Lake and one of the things that scared people in the area was the sound of the cougars or panthers. I remember two boys that were very much used to the dark as they were high school boys. They were coming across Third Lake from one house to the other, walking along. They heard a terrible screech beside them. They ran for the house, and they were scared. They had no idea what could have made the noise. I told them that it was probably a mountain lion as they don't roar or growl, they screech. They were really scared, the hair on their heads was standing on end... they were sure it was a ghost after them."

Now that story was the result of being in the dark woods, and an over-active imagination conjured up the fearful experience. However, what follows is the real thing and difficult to explain.

Greg continued saying, "Those boys may have thought ghosts were after them due to tales they'd heard from older guys who had read them in the Buffalo paper. In the 20's the 'Buffalo Sunday Times' used to come into Saint John as a Sunday paper. It had quite a few segments to it, and it was a big paper. It cost about 5 cents, back then. I remember there was quite a big article in it on Loch Lomond ghosts. This article struck me as very odd as the paper was from Buffalo, New York, but still had a story on a remote part of Saint John which was all forest and farmland- Loch Lomond. The stories told were ones about different ghostly experiences in that area. I can only remember one story vividly about a teamster driving his team to town who came to a bridge. I presume this is where the lake empties into the water pipes to town. At that point, the horses stopped. It was pitch black and the driver was surprised that the horses could find their way at all, but he kept them going until he came to the bridge. When the horses stopped dead, he tried to urge them on. He got off and found that the bridge had disappeared. The horses had sensed or could see that it was gone. That sure must have spooked the teamster and I bet that story was told around many cottage campfires after that," Greg laughed.

Digging deep into his memories Greg was able to recall another tale he'd been told. He believed it was likely widely shared, but asked that the family name be obscured, which I have done.

He said, "It was a Sunday afternoon and we were riding horses and such. In the evening, Father Burns came out, and we started telling ghost stories, each of us with our own idea of what a ghost story is about. Father Burns stopped us completely when he said that he had a story which was not a ghost story, but was a true story about his own experience with a devil in Loch Lomond. We listened up at that," Greg said. Father Burns continued, saying 'it was late one night, when I got a phone call that a man was dying and they requested a priest come and visit. The information I got was that it was one of the men in the McD..........family out at Loch Lomond. I started off, though I didn't know the territory well, but found my way to the McD.......... house. There were two families of McD's.............. The upper ones were quite a wild bunch of men and the lower McD's............. were a respectable family. The upper McD's............. were hard rock type. That's where the dying man was. When I went in the house, there was no one else in there except what I took to be the devil himself. He met me at the door and tried to keep me out. I was confident I could outmaneuver the devil, and I walked right in. When I got in the house the devil figure tried to outmaneuver me and push me around although the figure didn't dare touch me. I went past him and downstairs to where the dying man was, in the basement of the house. The devil still tried to separate me from him, but I continued to give the McD...............man the last rites of the church. When I finished, I left without a problem'."

Greg explained, "He told that story as a true account of what had happened, not as a ghost story. The priest said that he had never told the story previously, but given the circumstances at the party, he decided to tell us," Greg concluded.

Greg had many more stories that he shared of life in Saint John long ago, and of his younger days out around the lakes at Loch Lomond, but none of them were eerie in nature.

This devil spitting out coins is easy to spot on the Palatine building on Prince William Street in Saint John. Though no one knows exactly why it was chosen as the symbol for a bank, all can agree that it is not nearly as scary as the one the priest met out in Loch Lomond.

As a storyteller, it is often good to get in character when sharing tales, but, when I did this for a children's group, some would not come into the session, and when I was coming to the site of the storytelling on Canterbury Street, a gal I knew well crossed to the other side of the street thinking I was a nut case on the loose. Photo credit: Christy Bigney

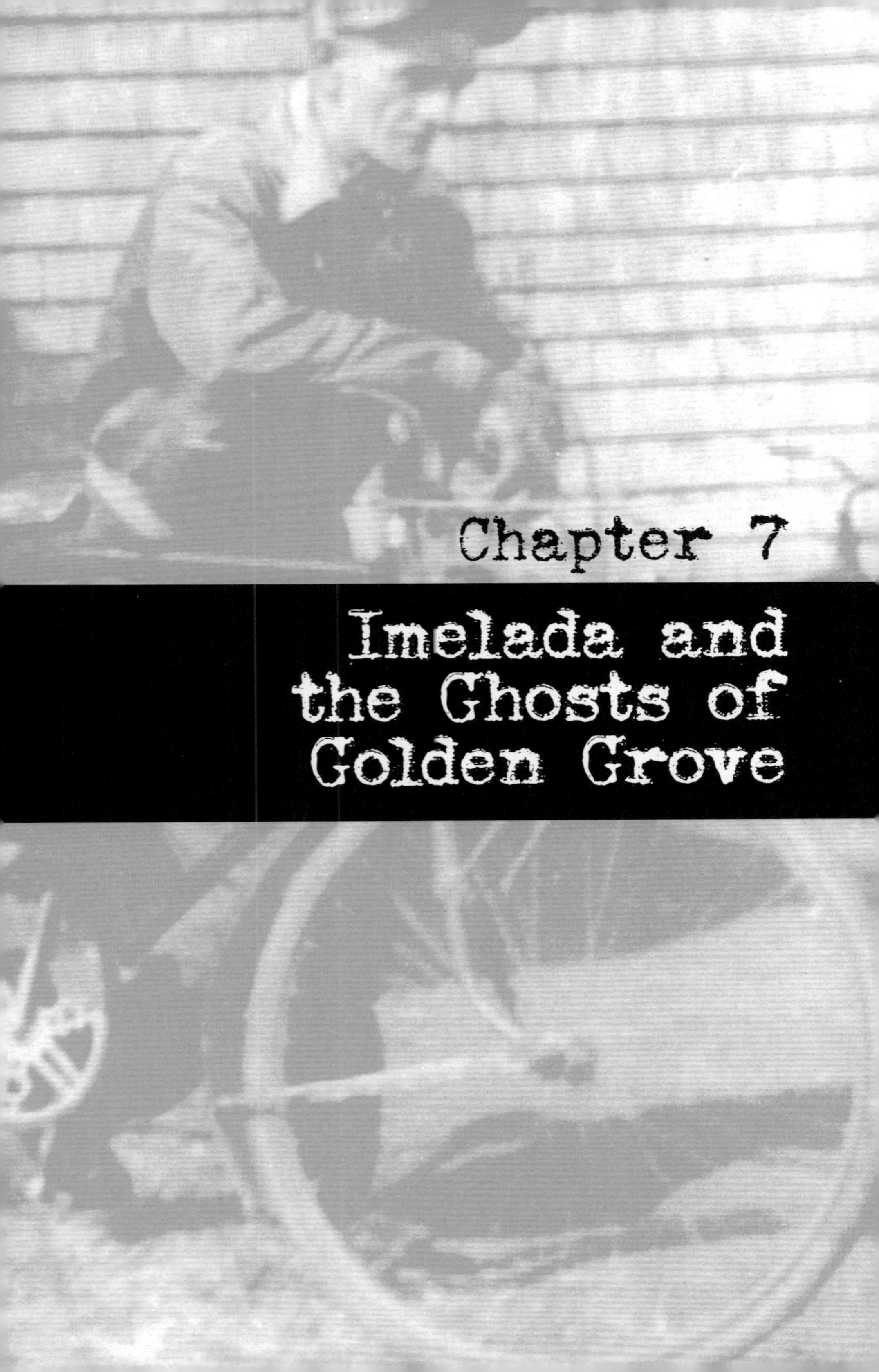

Chapter 7

Imelada and the Ghosts of Golden Grove

Imelada and the Ghosts of Golden Grove

Imelda Turner grew up in the fifties in the lake and hill country to the east of Saint John called Golden Grove. She recalls that it was an era when it seemed more country like than it does today. "Only a few of the residents had cars and only some of the homes were electrified," she said, adding "phones, found everywhere today, were sometimes miles down the road from where you lived."

She continued, "Everyone knew everyone else, and lent a helping hand when necessary. Storytelling was still widely practised," and Imelda, fortunately recalls those stories, and has been willing to share them. That inclination may be because she not only believed the tales she heard but had some strange experiences herself that she can share. So let's let her do just that.

"My great grandfather was Squire James Bowes. He built St. Patrick's Church in the Grove. He was a lawyer, a postmaster, and a carpenter. His son Edwin (Ned) was my grandfather. When Grandpa Ned was a young man the Squire was still alive and he had a big vegetable garden. He had grandfather load some of the crops on a wagon at harvest time to take to the City Market in town. Grandfather Ned was proceeding to town and when he reached the foot of Golden Grove Road, he noted workmen had been putting some new timbers on a bridge.

Grandfather had no way of knowing that earlier in the day a workman had been standing beside the bridge when the timbers spilled over and killed him. The man had been taken to a nearby inn and laid out in the upper room waiting for the coroner to come from Saint John to confirm that he was dead and that there had been no foul play.

As Grandfather Ned passed over the bridge, a young man stepped onto the roadway and asked him for a lift. They picked him up, got him comfortable in the second seat, and continued on toward town.

It was late in the day, so when they came to the inn, they decided to stay the night, and enjoy supper in the common room and some social time together.

They turned to tell their passenger that they were stopping for the night and he could hitch a ride to Saint John in the morning if he wanted to. They were surprised to find no passenger to speak to. Confused, they entered the inn and explained to the inn keeper that a fellow they had just picked up had just disappeared. The inn keeper beckoned them to follow him upstairs to the rooms. He showed them a bed with a man who appeared to be sleeping under a sheet. But when the inn keeper lifted up the sheet they were startled to see it was the lifeless body of the young fellow they had picked up. The inn keeper insisted that their tale was not possible as the dead man had been lying in the bed for several hours."

There was only one explanation, Imelda concluded, "It must have been the workman's ghost they picked up."

She continued her storytelling, saying: "There is a lonesome road which runs by St. Patrick's Church and joins the Dolan Road with the French Village Road. It was formerly called the 'Dam Road'. You can see that dam today behind the Irving station on the Dolan Road. It was a cold night and Grandfather Ned was coming from Rothesay when he came upon a man walking along the road with his hood up. Grandfather Ned stopped and asked whether the man would like a ride. He said he would, and he got up on the wagon. Being friendly, grandfather greeted the stranger and commented on the coldness of the night. The man didn't reply; he didn't say a word. Grandfather thought maybe the fellow was not a talker so he didn't bother the stranger. They went down the Dam Road and as they got to the French Village Road the fellow jumped off. Grandfather said to him 'You're not going any further? I can take you further.' The stranger looked up at grandfather and where there should have been a face beneath the hood there was just a dark black void."

Imelda told of another incident involving a Grove resident named Halsie Atkins. "He was a bit eccentric. He drove a bike summer and winter. One winter day he was coming into town on his bike and had to get off because it was snowing very hard. He noticed that there were footprints appearing in the snow beside him. But no one was there, just footprints keeping pace beside him."

The stories about Halsie got around and led to some people having what others thought was an overactive imagination- but Imelda does not think it was imagination at all, for she was there to witness the incident that follows.

"There was this fellow father knew who worked the night shift in the late 50's. Once he was coming by car out the road after working all night and he was very tired and falling asleep at the wheel. He decided to pull over and have a sleep on the French Village Road. He stopped near the grave yard of St. Patrick's Church. He had a nice snooze but woke up with a start. He reached for the key to start the car. He looked out the windshield, and was alarmed to see fingers coming down over the glass as though someone on the roof was trying to come down over the car. The fingers were transparent. He was kind of stunned, and as he sat there the top of a head started to come down from the roof of the car to join the transparent hands. That was enough. He jumped out of the car and ran through St. Patrick's graveyard, through the swamp and out to the Grove Road where he ended up banging on our door. I can still remember that he was totally scared to death. He told dad than he didn't believe in what he'd seen, but explained it just as it had happened. Father calmed him down, and then took him to retrieve the car. When they got there, there was no sign that anything unusual had happened."

Something had scared the fellow, and Imelda believed the story then and still does, and you would too if what follows happened to you as it did to Imelda.

Imelda's Grandfather Ned's homestead was abandoned after he died. Imelda had warm memories of the place and decided to spend a night there with two friends. Imelda recounted the incident saying, "It was Neville Wissmann and Brenda Cairns, and we dragged mattresses over to the upstairs room for the night. Around three a.m. we awoke for no apparent reason. We nudged one another and we were a little scared. 'Are you awake?' I said softly into the darkness. 'Yes, are you?' said Neville. She was the big cousin. Brenda heard us and said, 'Are you two awake? Listen. What woke us all up?' We couldn't hear anything. There was silence; deep, deep silence. Then there were steps, stilted steps. We thought the steps were the neighbourhood boys though the sounds were heavier than a boy's would be. It sounded like someone was making a determined effort to get to the top of the landing. When they got there, they turned and came left down the hall towards us. As we heard the sound of the steps pass in the hallway, a fog or a mist shape filled the open doorway. We could see it and feel it. Neville still thought it was the boys. She got up and went out into the hallway, but she soon came back. The step sound then proceeded along the top of the landing and again past the doorway. Neville waited for it to happen again. When the step sound stopped she went out in the hall, leaned over the railing and hollered, 'Boys, don't think you're going to scare us!' The footsteps stopped. Then the three of us got back in bed and the footsteps started again. After two more times we'd had enough, and decided to leave. We didn't see or hear anyone as we went down the same stairs where we had heard the footsteps. It took a lot of courage for us to do that. We felt watched, but we didn't dare look back. At the end of the driveway, though, I got brave and glanced back. No wonder we felt watched, for I saw a figure in the window...a figure of a man wearing a hat."

Imelda wondered about that figure for years.

Recently, she was sent a photo of her Grandfather Ned, and to her surprise, he was wearing the very hat she'd seen on the figure in the window.

"It makes sense," she admits, "After all, it was his house."

As teenagers Imelda and her friends had no desire to have a sleepover in that house again, nor does she to this day.

The photo shows Ned and Bessie Bowes, Imelda's grandparents. It was given to Imelda as an adult and it was not until then that she realized it was probably her grandfather's ghost stomping on the stairs that spooked her while overnighting at his old home when she was a teenager. Photo Credit Imelda Turner

Halsie Atkins and the bicycle he often rode. Photo Credit Imelada Turner

Chapter 8

The Lower Cove Specter

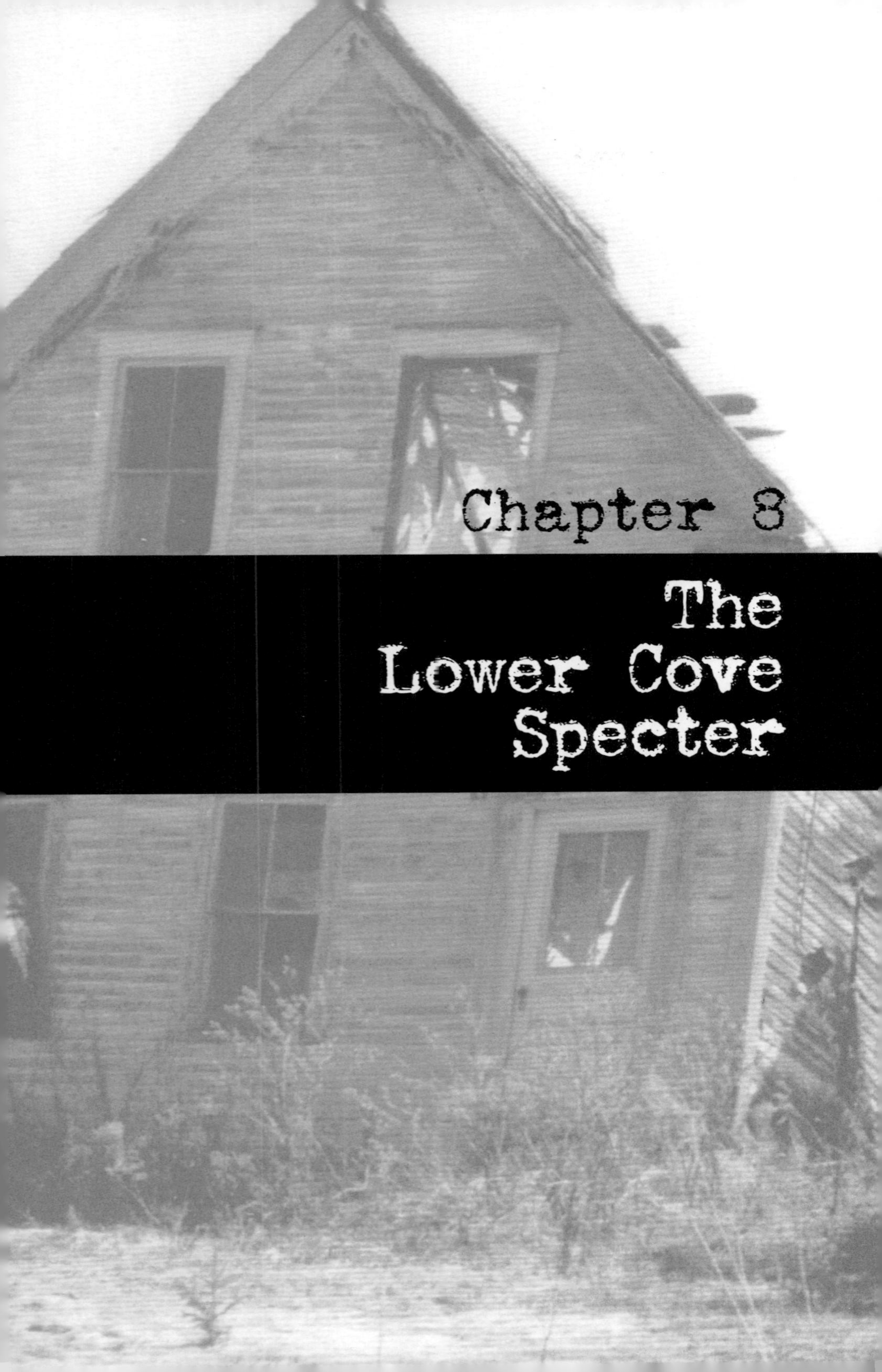

The Lower Cove Specter

For the next few chapters, we move to the city, and share stories from uptown Saint John and the North and South End. We begin with the latter:

This story of a husband who came all the way from Nova Scotia to haunt his wife on Saint John's Britain Street at the end of the 19th century is the most documented ghost story of any I have seen to date. In fact, there is so much background, that I can give but a taste of it in this chapter. Anyone whose appetite is whetted and wants all the nitty gritty details can drop by the Saint John library and look up the story in all four newspapers that were publishing at the time the event occurred in November of 1889, namely the "Saint John Globe," the "Saint John Daily Sun," the "Saint John Daily Telegraph", and the weekly "Progress" from which I have summarized the following tale.

It begins with a Mr. John Jackson and his wife Mary, then living in Hantsport, Nova Scotia. John died in the fall of 1887 and his wife moved to Saint John. She took up residence in what was described as a small, one story cottage on the east end of Britain Street, that contained three rooms, these being two bed chambers, separated by a kitchen.

It was in the front chamber, overlooking the street that Mary began to encounter the spirit of her dead husband. It seems he came to visit with some regularity, but she did not share details of these visits with anyone for months and months. Finally, the visits troubled her so much that she moved a few blocks and stayed with her friend Mrs. Mary Anderson. At that point, they called in a minister of the gospel, a Rev. Wm. Lawson, to the Britain Street house to verify it was indeed being haunted. However, Rev. Lawson did not experience a ghost on his visit to the house, which cast doubt on Mary's story.

The two ladies then appealed to Methodist Evangelist, Rev. H. S. Hartley to make a visit. At first, he too was skeptical and declined, but upon being asked a second time, he agreed to come to the house after the Sunday evening prayer service. After offering Mrs. Jackson some advice to the effect that she should lead a righteous life, he read the well known 23rd Psalm, "The Lord is my Shepherd," in English, and another unnamed psalm in Latin. He then said a few prayers, and entered the house. Up to that point, the Daily Telegraph noted "he had noticed nothing unusual." However, the story continues, and went on to say that when the minister entered the front bedroom, "he plainly saw the form of a man lying there." To "examine the mystery," he moved toward the bed. To his surprise, the form moved, and was next observed sitting up in a chair beside the bed. At that point Mr. Hartley "attempted to touch him, [and] the apparition, so it seemed, moved off, passed through the kitchen, approached the cupboard, [and] vanished."

Following Hartley's visit, many neighbours came to peek into the windows of the house, including the widow, who would not return to the house to live. Many observers were interviewed by the press and claimed to have seen the form of what his widow was sure was her dead husband, lying on the bed. Some visitors said they had seen lights move about within the vacant structure, and others said they noticed a strange smell coming from the abode and spoke of an "oppressive atmosphere," around the house.

Hartley arranged a second visit for the following night, and to legitimize what he had seen, decided to bring the police along. Out of some 50 spectators gathered at the scene, twenty were selected to go into the house to look for the ghost of Jackson. At first, it seemed there were too many present for the ghost to make an appearance. Though many attempts were made to coax the ghost out through the singing of hymns, and the offering of prayers, Jackson's spirit did not put in an appearance. Then the crowd thinned out, and some in the house got discouraged and left. But not all went away, for just after one o'clock, a man alone in the front bedroom had the experience of the bedroom door shutting him in, and this was followed by a rapping on the floor, and the appearance of a figure on what had been a vacant bed. He immediately called the others in the house, but by the time they got there no ghost was to be seen. However the bedclothes had been disturbed where the form had lain.

Sure by then that there was something strange occurring, Rev. Hartley agreed to a "laying of the ghost." To carry that ceremony off, he charged the widow Jackson $2.00 just to make it "legal," and made her a promise he would send her husband, John Jackson, "back to the spirit world."

However, he failed to do so and Mrs. Jackson was unable to move back into the house, as she claimed her pastor friend had failed to get her dead husband out of the house.

Unfortunately, that is where the tale ends in the papers of the day. What became of the ghost of John Jackson is unknown. Did he continue to haunt his wife Mary Jackson? Did she continue to live with her friend or did she remarry and live happily somewhere else? The details are not known. What became of the tiny house on Britain Street where the living and dead interacted also remains a mystery. No further reports of what was termed the "Lower Cove Specter" were found in any of the papers publishing at the time, nor has any light been shed on the matter in the reading of many ghostly encounters in Saint John's papers over the years since the incident.

Perhaps, just perhaps, someone reading this does know the rest of the story...someone who lives in a small cottage on Britain Street or what has been built up around that cottage, and the person and will come forward with the rest of the story of the ghost of John Jackson.

This is not the house on Britain Street- no picture exists of it, but whenever a house falls into disrepair, as is the case here, there are always stories that circulate about the possibility of it being haunted. This house, located at Johnville, New Brunswick, was considered a haunted house, as, over the years many people saw what seemed to be a ghostly figure of a man peering out from the second floor windows when they came to the field adjacent the building to pick blueberries.

Chapter 9

Strange Occurrences at the Venerable Imperial Theatre that are not Readily Explainable

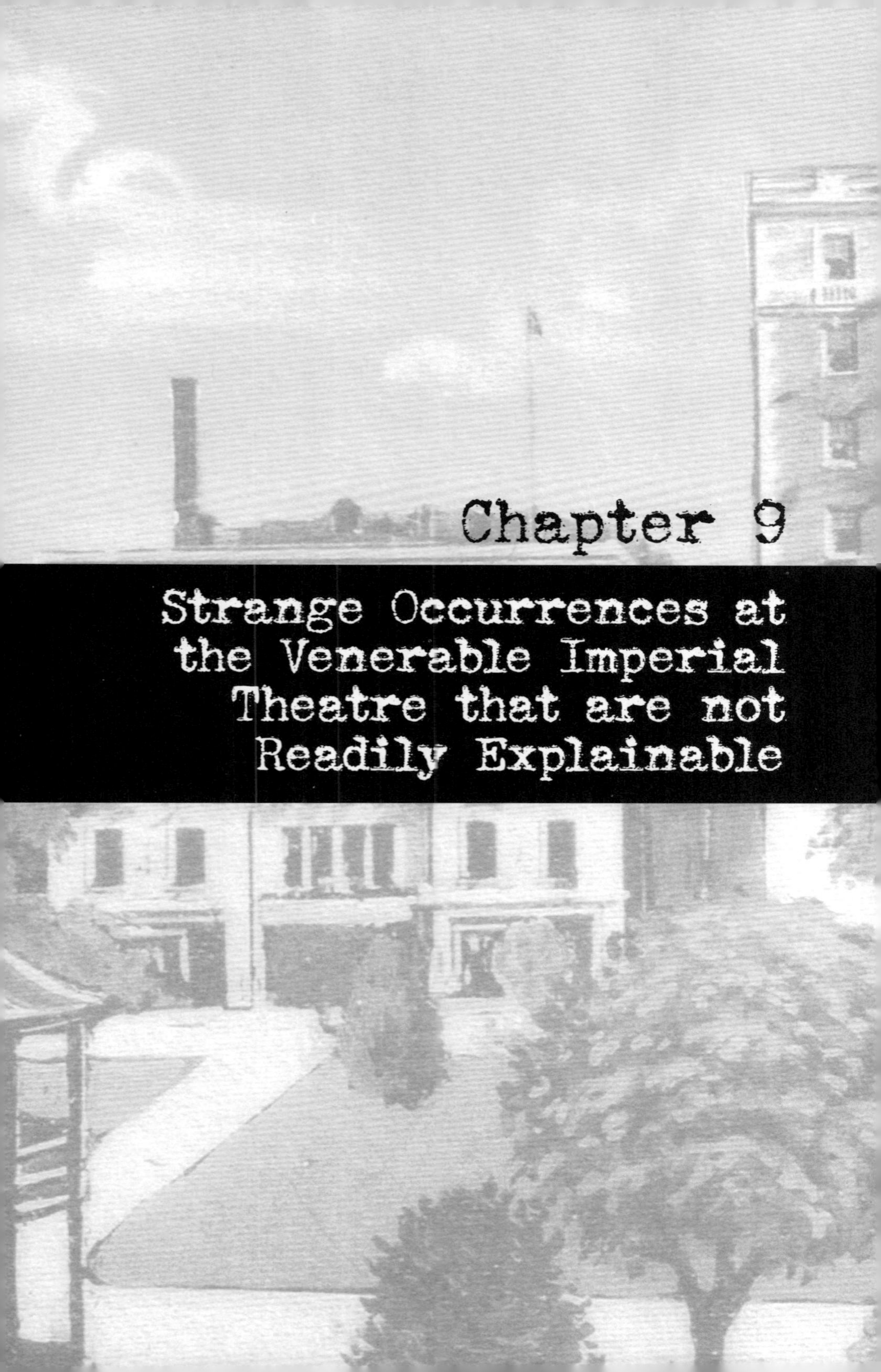

Strange Occurrences at the Venerable Imperial Theatre that are not Readily Explainable

The Imperial Theatre on King's Square south is not only one of Canada's top performing arts centers...(some say it's the best!), but it is also one of the country's oldest, as it celebrated its 100th birthday in 1913.

It was largely through the efforts of the manager of the Nickel Theatre, which began showing moving pictures at just five cents a show in 1907, that we have the Imperial Theatre to enjoy all these years later.

Walter H. Golding was that manager, and he conceived the idea of having Santa Claus attend afternoon matinees to complement the showing of Clement Clark Moore's 'Twas the Night Before Christmas. In the days before Santa was not the ubiquitous figure he is now, this combination packed the theatre day after day with children anxious to see the portly saint and enjoy a movie and a live play in which Santa was the star. Just as in Moore's story, Santa emerged from a fireplace, and not only interacted with the personages on stage in a short skit, but came into the audience to pass out candy to the children.

The success of Golding's presentations, called a "big source of delight," by the media of the day, made him bold enough to suggest to the Keith Albee Corporation of New York, owners of the Nickel, that they should build a grand New York Style theatre in the city. "We don't build in the sticks," was the American company's response.

Undeterred, the following Christmas Golding added live orchestral music to the program mix. He was told by the New York owners to give the musicians a week's notice and get rid of them. He refused and within six months, every theatre in America copied his idea, and all had live orchestras to compliment the vaudeville acts and movie shorts they were presenting.

For Christmas 1908, Golding augmented Santa's role by having him collect letters from the children present. On entering the theatre the children were also encouraged to deposit ballots in the lobby from which Santa would draw names and awarded prizes donated by local merchants. "The Nickel is the storehouse of pure amusement for the little ones at vacation time," said the Daily Telegraph.

In 1913, the Nickel added, "another epoch making invention," namely, the "kinetophone," which was described as a "talking moving picture." When it was demonstrated, hundreds were turned away from each show, according to the Daily Telegraph's account of the event on May 6, 1913.

By then, the Keith Albee concerns had changed their mind about Saint John being unable to support a full size theatre, and the Imperial was in the last stages of being built on the lot on which is stands to this day overlooking King's Square. It opened on September 19, 1913.

Golding continued to manage the theatre, and the Christmas shows with Santa, and various musical and novelty acts continued to be part of the theatre's mix of presentations until the late 30's.

Golding wrote many accounts of the early days of theatre in the city, and of his own experiences living in an apartment in the Imperial from 1913 until his death in 1945. He summed up his life just three years before his death in an interview with Stuart Trueman but in that interview, and in other accounts he penned, he makes no mention of ghosts or spirits that dwelt with him in his beloved Imperial.

However, there are those who say they do exist, and as it is common for theatres across the county to have unexplained happenings and ghostly occurrences, why should we doubt the accounts which follow collected from persons who have spent many an hour in the confines of the glorious Imperial Theatre?

The storytellers are Mike Horobin and Darik Hatfield, who experienced the ghosts while employees of the theatre, and Marilyn Williams, who has played there as much as any other musician in Saint John and has heard a good many tales of the unexplained from those she has worked with.

Darik shared the stories when I was the Master of Ceremonies for the 3rd Field Regiment and St. Mary's Band concert in October 2009. Darik had taken employment elsewhere by the time I followed up on his tales, but I was fortunate in being able to speak to Mike Horrobin and Marilyn Williams, who told me basically what Darik had shared with me.

Mike said, "It's a big old building, and there has been a lot of passion on the stage and among the members of the audience for a century. When a show finishes, the empty building cools at different rates, and I feel that might account for some of the noises I have heard late at night as we were finishing up after a show."

He added, "I have been in the building and heard someone walk across the attic area. There is about 12 feet of space between the ornamented ceiling and the roof. No one would be up there after the show yet, I have heard footsteps go right across the ceiling right over where the audience would sit."

To that he added, "I have been in the building when I have smelled smoke, as if someone was smoking, and have had a distinct odour of perfume that wafted across the stage when I was in there, all alone, after a show."

This should not happen, Mike claims, and by way of explanation he said, "The theatre has the 2nd largest air exchange system in Saint John, and if someone was smoking anywhere in the building, it could get sucked into the system. Also, people smoke outside in the alley, do drugs, etc, so it could get sucked in. That could explain it, but how do you explain the perfume odor? Where would that come from?" Mike asked, obviously in belief that there was an otherworldly explanation for the phenomena he experienced.

Marilyn added to Mike's story with one about Jim Wilson who told her of hearing voices calling his name to the point that he would go to the office to see if they were paging him.

"But they weren't," she said and added, "Jim told me it happened more than once," and he was left wondering if someone was playing the trick on him, or was there some other reason for the calls he could distinctly hear. Ghosts? Who knows," Marilyn said.

The theatre has a very elaborate sound system and its own sound booth, which Darik Hatfield talked of when I chatted with him. He said, "In the sound booth, there are large vertical plastic baffles to absorb the sound and keep it from bouncing around. These are heavy and not supposed to move no matter what. I was in the sound booth, and the baffles opened up enough that I'm sure someone was walking through them. But the sound booth is 40 feet up over the stage...no one can walk on air...yet, the baffles open just enough to indicate a human presence was walking through them. If it happened once, well, I'd dismiss it, but it happened more than a few times and each time it happened, there was a great chill that filled the room. These rooms are air tight, and locked so that they are not accessible to anyone except the sound man," Darik explained.

Not everything happens behind the stage, over the stage, or late at night, according to the three interviewees. Mike said, "The front office staff have had regular visits from a young girl who seems willing to help them, but no one knows who she is, or where she comes from, and she does not stick around to explain." Mike noted, "This is the oldest part of the building and has always been the ticket taking area," then added, "Perhaps the girl is one of the ticket takers that Mr. Walter Golding employed. He was so convinced that a theatre would work in Saint John he was determined to show the Keith Albee Company of New York that their building in the sticks was as wise decision. He worked hard himself, and expected others to work hard too. Perhaps one of those he employed is still trying to do her job at the office," Mike speculated.

As the theatre has moved into its second hundred years of operation all three of those interviewed are sure it will continue to be valued as Saint John's leading cultural centre, and they are also convinced that ghostly presences will continue to be part of the show.

And they are not the only ones who hold this opinion. On October 31, of 2013, the Loyalist City Paranormal group, led by Diana Grant, spent the night in the Imperial to see if they could make any contact with any spirits lurking in the theatre. While their results were inconclusive, one filmed segment clearly shows the laws of nature being stretched on the stage. A medicine ball was placed there, and camera's focused on it through the night. It remained staticnery for a long time, then, suddenly, it moved three feet or so to the left, then zigged forward, and stopped. Then, after a short delay, it returned to its original position, where it remained for the rest of the night. Members of the group are still seeking an explanation for that, and for voices and footsteps recorded on their sensitive "ghost hunting equipment." As well, like Mike Horrobin, many there that night said they detected the odour of smoke, as if there was a fire burning somewhere in the building. This included your scribe, who had joined the group for part of the night curious to see if the many stories he's been told had any credulence.

Over the decades, the 1925 Admiral Beatty Hotel and the 1913 Imperial Theatre (known as the Capitol in this postcard image) have been objects of interest on any visit to King's Square. Though several ghostly encounters can be told about the theatre, none seem to exist about the former hotel, though hotels usually do have such stories.

Chapter 10

North End Ghosts

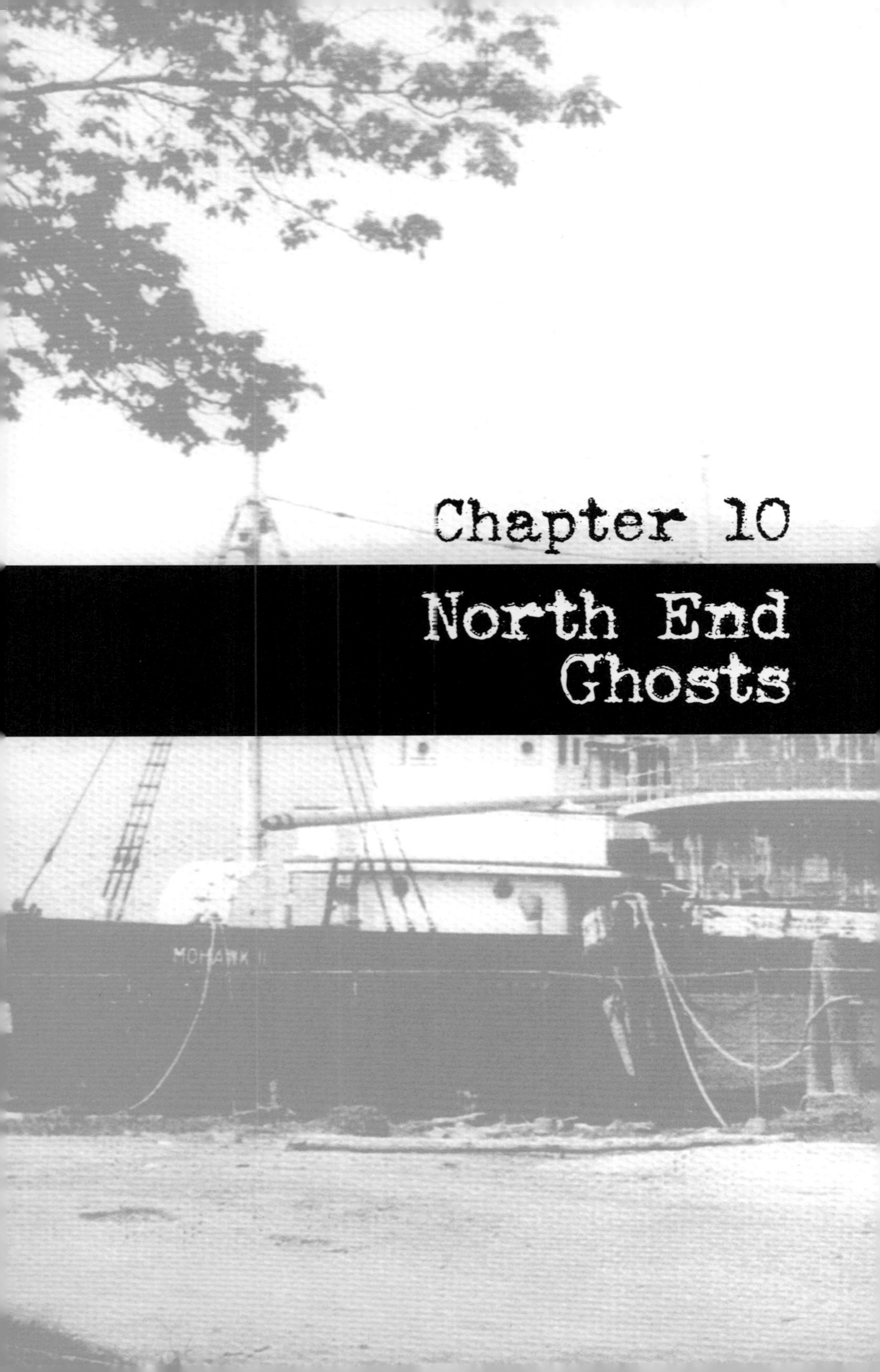

North End Ghosts

I decided early on to make sure that every area of the city was represented in the tales recounted in this book.

Fortunately, it has not been a difficult task as every area has more than one story, and in some areas, like the old North End, there were many possibilities to choose from.

In times past, the North End of Saint John would be defined by most people as the area surrounding Main Street and Victoria Street running north and south, and located between the St. John River and Douglas Avenue. Some might expand these parameters a bit to include all of Main Street up to the Viaduct, and the houses of Simonds and High Streets that existed before urban renewal of the 60's. Others would add the Portland Place, Rifle Range area, and the perhaps the former Shamrock Park. All this area was tightly packed with residents until fifty years ago, and ghost tales were among the stories they shared when there were Saturday night card and kitchen parties.

Most residents of the area would claim that the imposing Count DeBury House opposite St Luke's church was haunted. It sure looks like it might be. Some might even repeat an oft told story that there are tunnels between the Count's house and the sea captain's houses on Douglas Avenue long known as Blue Boy and Pinky. Today, the houses are joined and serve as an upscale Bed& Breakfast known as Homeport. No tunnels exist, according to current owners of both properties nor are either bothered by ghosts.

Across the street from the Homeport B&B at 41 Douglas Avenue, was the home of Isaac Oulton, known to North Enders as "Old Holt, the Miser" because he lived hermit-like in a ramshackle house between Main St. and Clarendon St. from 1839 until he was murdered in April 1902. His unfortunate murder was supposedly motivated by stories that a huge amount of cash was hidden in his house. The basis of the belief he had money hidden away were accounts he often told locals of having struck it rich in the gold rush of 1849 in California. Secondly, numismatists in the city spread the story of his wealth based on an interview with Holt that appeared in a "Coin Collector's Magazine" which stated he had a fortune of old coins worth about $50,000.

Holt, miserly in his ways, scavenged daily for food at the Metcalfe Street dump, and when his wife died, he wheeled her body out Douglas Avenue in a wheelbarrow rather than hire a wagon to take her to Cedar Hill Cemetery. These actions added further credence to the belief he had money, and that he had stashed it somewhere in the clutter of his old house instead of placing it the banks, which, as he often told people, he distrusted.

Who killed him was never discovered. What is evident though is that just after he was murdered the police guarding the crime scene had quite a scare. On May 7, 1902 the "Daily Sun" headline asked, "Is it haunted? Queer stories about Oulton's House- A Policeman's scare."

The article went on to recount how those passing the boarded up house had seen "flickering lights" and heard "muffled moans" emanating from the inside of the house. Policeman, however, claimed they had not seen or heard such things. However, one officer had quite a scare one night. He reported, "It was about three o'clock in the morning, and the street lights were out. I was standing in a doorway across the road from the house and was watching when I heard a faint footfall approaching from the entrance of the Avenue (Douglas Avenue). Up the road, in the dim light, came the bent over figure of an old man. On his bowed back he was carrying a bag. The helmet of his cap raised up on his bristling hair and his eyes *started. "(Authors note: This is likely "*stared", but it is printed as started.)

The officer wrote in his report, that he thought "it's old man Oulton coming back from the dark." He was about to flee when to his relief, he found it was not Oulton at all, but a man who looked a lot like him; a mason carrying a sack over his back just as Oulton was known to do. Upon approaching the fellow, the policeman learned he had been heading off to

Manawagonish Road for an early morning job.

No doubt others saw the fellow too, and his Oulton- like appearance ensured the rumours persisted that the miser was keeping watch over his treasure in the old house. No treasure was found, though, but what did come to light in the house was a treasure chart of the Little River area at Courtenay Bay, and this led to many hours of searching in the vicinity of the old Poor House on Bayside Drive, and indeed some Spanish Doubloons were found there. But not $50,000 and what happened to that remains a mystery, as does the question of whether it was Oulton's ghost being seen, or was there some logical explanation for what was sighted at the old house following his murder.

Besides the story of Lady Latour's ghost, found in chapter one of this collection, there are three other stories of ghosts in the area and all are short and lack great detail but they are still worth mentioning.

One story is about happenings at the former Sourisky's Store on Rockland Road and a presence which tormented the daughter of the family by eerily calling her name repeatedly. Although unseen, the forceful creature threw fire around the house and one time kicked a boarder on his backside to drive him out of the house. Certainly this was the meanest ghost I've ever heard of in Saint John. The storyteller, who wished anonymity, did not know how the family got rid of the ghost, though she was sure they did as they lived there until Urban Renewal took the properly in the 60's.

Another story involved a widower living on Newman Street who had been left with two young children when his wife died, and who had taken a new wife before she was even cold in the grave. To the new couple's surprise, the deceased wife came to their flat each night to tuck her children in at bedtime. It is surmised she did not think much of the second wife's sudden appearance in the home, and in her child rearing ability!

The third story is even more fragmentary, as after tweaking my interest about a noisy ghost on Bridge Street, the family decided they would rather not share the tale after all.

So, in replacement of the story I can't tell you, I recently came across another ghostly encounter in the North End and got permission to tell it from the storyteller.

I learned the tale when a youth group associated with the social action group, "One Change" in the North End of Saint John called and asked for a ghost walk for their members on the day before Hallowe'en.

I accepted the job with trepidation, as I knew I had only a bit of local lore to share of the area.

Beyond what you've read here, I knew I was going to have to fall back on widely known generic ghost tales, and tell them as if they had happened locally. For instance, I figured I could use the most famous of all ghost stories, the tale of the man who picks up a female hitchhiker in the driving rain, and when he reaches her home, she has disappeared from the back seat. But the seat is still soaked, so he knows he did pick up someone! I could tell the youngster's the tale and say it happened right in the North End. This usually works just fine.

Another story that is always good for the youth is the tale of a young couple out parking and enjoying some tunes when they hear on the radio that there is a murderer, known by a hook on his hand, on the loose in the city. The lady insists she be driven home. Once there, she insists he open her door and escort her to her house. When he reaches for the door handle, a hook is stuck to the car.

I knew this story could also be told as if it happened at St. Peter's Park, or Lily Lake, and when this is done, it usually sends a chill up the spines of the listeners.

And there are a few more tales of similar nature; however, I did not need to localize the two well known "urban legends" above, as one of the participants provided the thrill of the evening with a tale I had never heard about the area.

To localize the story he told, think of Main Street, and how it terminates at the St. John River just after it has flowed through the Pokiok Narrows, and just before it flows into the Reversing Falls.

For a good portion of the city's history, this area, known locally as Indiantown, was a busy industrial zone, and the terminus of the riverboat service. Thousands of people were crammed into the tenements on the hills overlooking the river, and a tiny beach among the busy wharves was their only place for a summer dip. On at least one occasion, a swim turned tragic, as a young man named Jason told us that night. Here is his story:

"A girl drowned in the St. John River at Indiantown at the north end of Main Street. There is a popular hangout for teens overlooking the site of her drowning. Kids would often gather there to enjoy one another's company, swing, and play games. A rumour spread among the youth that if you called the drowned young girl's name three times, you would hear her splashing in the water, which perhaps was the sound of her last frantic moments as she was drowning. Two young girls went down to the area one night. They arrived in a van, but didn't bother to lock it as they would only be a few feet away in the park. While they were sitting on the swings, one girl said to the other.

'Do you remember the drowning that happened in the river out there?'

The other girls said she did, as it had only been a few years earlier and she had heard her parents and other friends talk about it.

'Well,' said the first girl, 'I've heard that if you call the drowned girl's name, you will hear her splashing out there.'

'Naw, that can't happen,' the second girl said.

The first girl responded, 'Well, I know the girl's name, it was Emily, so why don't we try it and see what happens.'

'I don't think that is a good idea,' the second girl said, 'I don't think you should play around with things like that.'

'Aw, come on,' the first girl said, 'The van is right behind us. We can run right up to it if anything happens.'

'Well, okay,' said the second girl, 'but I am getting my sneakers back on, and getting ready to run if anything happens.'

'Now we have to do this together,' the first girl said, 'I'll say one, two three, and we will call her name, okay?'

'Yes, let's do it,' the second girl said.

And so they did.

'One, two three,' the first girl said softly, and then both of them shouted, 'Emily!'

Nothing happened.

The first girl said, 'I've heard you have to do it three times, so let's do it again. Ready, one, two three.'

And they shouted the second time, 'Emily!'

'Just as they say,' the first girl said, 'It will take three times.'

But the second girl said, 'I thought I heard something...sounded like a little gurgle out there in the dark. Didn't you hear it?'

'No,' said the first girl. 'Now I will say one, two, and three again, and we'll see what happens.'

The second girls said, 'I...I...I... don't want to....I... I.... I... think I heard something. Don't do it.'

But the first girl shouted, 'Emily!' at the top of her lungs.

And a voice out on the water came back, saying, 'Help me, Help! Help!' and there was a gurgling and splashing of water out in the dark over the river.

Girl two looked at girl one, and without hesitation they both jumped up and scurried over the grass to the van.

To their great surprise, it was locked with the keys inside. And they could still hear the sound of splashing in the water…and Emily calling 'Help! Help!'

Of course, they got away from there as quickly as they could, abandoning the van, which they recovered the next morning when the sun came up, and they were no longer frightened of the area.

You can bet those two never went back again at night though, but lots of other teens have…and you might try calling Emily yourself some night. If you do, be sure you lock your car, and know where your keys are!" Jason concluded.

Despite the heavy industrial nature of the Indiantown area, local residents would take to the water in a sandy cove to the left of the tug in what is now called Robertson's Square…sometimes to their regret.

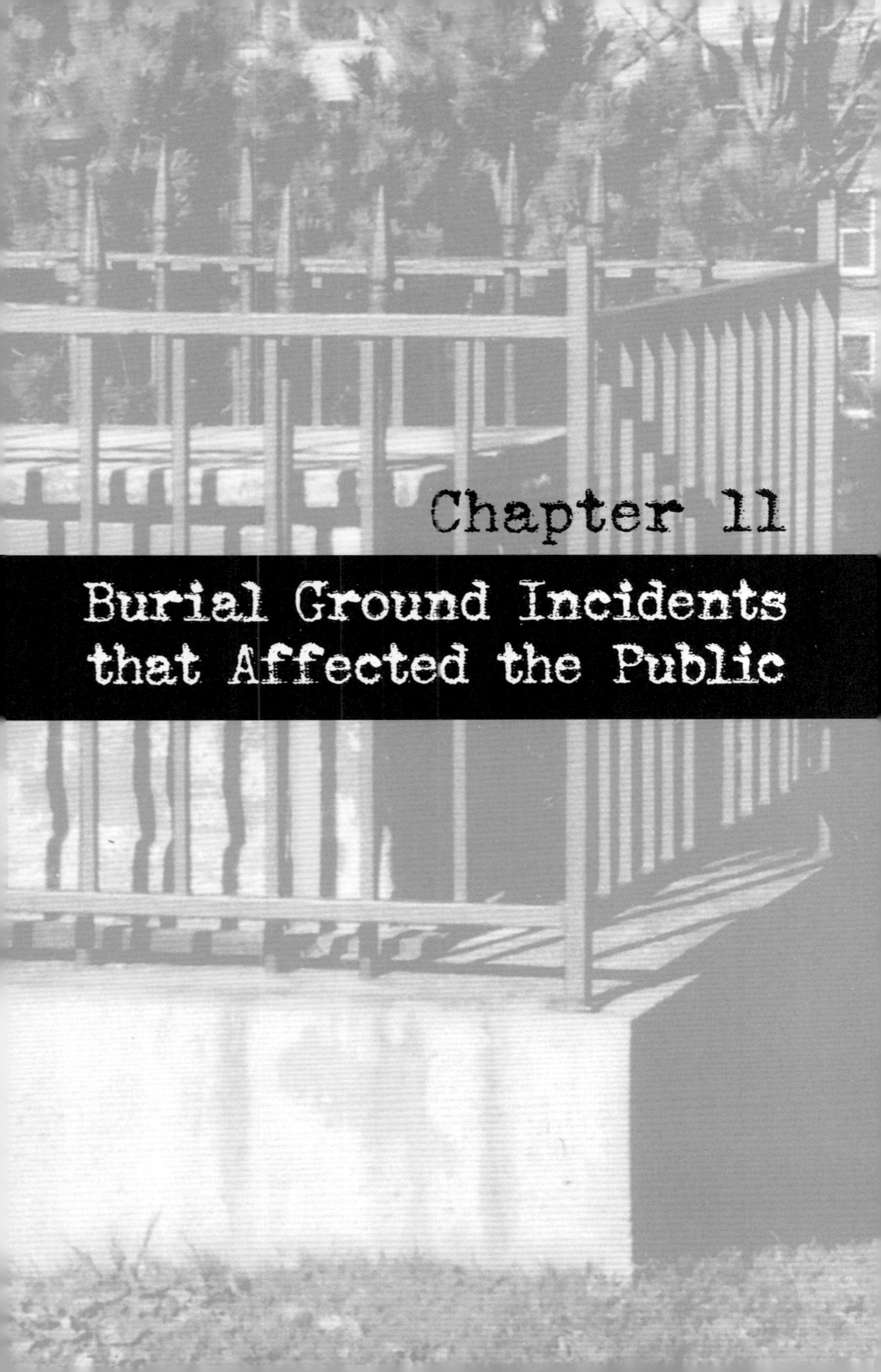

Chapter 11

Burial Ground Incidents that Affected the Public

Burial Ground Incidents that Affected the Public

Saint Johners have had several unusual experiences in some of the thirteen burial sites that have been in use in the city in its just over 400 years of settlement counting from the days of the La Tours at Portland Point in the 1640's.

One morning after I had led a walking tour of the Cedar Hill Cemetery on the west side, I got a call from a man who had a story to relate. I encouraged him to share it, and I listened with open ears as he began his story: "Late one night I was taking a shortcut through the Cedar Hill graveyard," he began, "and about midpoint, I heard the most awful thrashing about and moaning and groaning coming from the dark recesses of a freshly dug grave. I didn't hang around to see what was making the noise. When I got home, I could not blot out the noise. I lived behind Beaconsfield School, so I was a good half mile from the graveyard. I closed my windows; I put a pillow over my head and I pulled the covers over too, but the moaning kept me awake all night. At dawn I got the courage to return to the cemetery, and look into the grave. All was quiet as I approached the hole, and it was only when I looked in that I found that a cow had wandered from the adjacent pasture and fallen in the grave. By morning the cow had given up its struggle until she saw me peer in. Immediately she started the thrashing and clawing and moaning I'd heard the night before, the most dreadful sounds you could imagine. Well, the farmer came and got her out and just in time, as there was a hearse approaching from Lancaster Avenue. Can you imagine the grieving family upon hearing that moaning?" he laughed.

I laughed too, and have since used his story to good effect dozens of times when passing through that graveyard on walking tours.

But not all macabre happenings in that cemetery were laughable. Indeed not, for back in 1888 on the Sunday afternoon of June 16, a cluster of boys playing among the hardwoods adjacent to the cemetery made the discovery of a pile of decaying bones and the broken remains of several coffins in the undergrowth. Soon all of the West Side of the city was in a tizzy thinking their loved ones resting in the cemetery had been visited by grave robbers, which was still a common occurrence at the time. An investigation ensued and it was soon discovered that the caretaker had been ill, and had turned the grave digging job over to his son. Not knowing, as his dad did, just where people were buried, he dug up former burials in the process of making space for the newly dead. Rather than dig another hole, he simply hid the remains of formerly buried bodies and older coffins in the nearby woods. Both men lost their jobs, and the community settled down once again upon knowing there were no creepy capers going on in the Carleton cemetery.

Not far from this location is the Tower Hill Cemetery, so named as it is overlooked by Martello Tower. Originally it was the burial place of most Roman Catholics in Saint John west, but eventually it was full, and a second cemetery opened up on Sand Cove Road known as Holy Cross. It is still in use, and though Tower Hill fell into disrepair, it has been refurbished, and makes an interesting place to visit.

One visitor Thomas Yandall caused quite a commotion back on May 21 of 1887. He was living in Sussex when he learned a friend, J. O'Donnell had died. He walked to Saint John, and easily found his friend's marker in the Tower Hill cemetery. He wanted to have one last look at him, so he dug him up! However, when he left the scene he didn't rebury the body of his friend, but left it lying on the grass. Three young boys came along soon after, and upon discovering the remains, told their parents what they had found. The news spread like wildfire and soon all the Catholics in Carleton were coming to see if it was a family member that was laying there. What they saw was unidentifiable, it being a six year old cadaver, which by then was basically a skeleton. An investigation followed. It was declared that Yandall was, as was said then, "feeble minded," and thus, no charges could be laid.

Our final cemetery story is an abridged account of a late night meeting in the old Burial Ground on Sydney Street as recorded by a reporter of the "Morning News" of June 24, 1906 under the title, "A Midnight Meeting in the Old Burial Ground."

"An unusual congregation gathered in the south-east corner of the old burial ground last night....

At midnight the meeting was called to order by one of the older members rapping sharply on a dilapidated tombstone with his bony heel....

With an effort the honoured skeleton gathered himself together and addressed the assembly: 'Ladies and gentlemen, ancestors of the descendants of the Loyalists, founders of the City of Saint John..... You are called together to discuss a grave question....It has come to our notice that the present generation, seeking after a place for amusement, contemplates ...locating a band stand in this place, formerly our property and supposed to be sacred to our memory. Apparently it was thought that we were too dead to raise any objection...This is a lamentable state of affairs and it remains for us to make some move in the matter. I would like to have an expression of opinion from the meeting.'

After a short pause a gentleman arose who had lost a portion of his anatomy during the building of one of the walks. He cleared his throat and remarked; 'We never objected when children played on our tombstones and tourists broke off portions for mementos. We never even made a remark about using the place as a pound for all the stray and unlicensed dogs, but this latest move is too much-too much. I had hopes that some of our descendants would remonstrate, but I fear they are too busy organizing Loyalist societies. I enter my unqualified objections to the whole affair.'

The speaker had scarcely finished when another got up and remarked: 'My resting place is in the North West corner of this lot, and I have had my own troubles there. My headstone has been used by workmen to sharpen their implements, and I am opposed to the opening of any music stand in this vicinity. It would be but the opening wedge for some members of a minstrel troupe to come in and play the bones. We must nip this movement in the bud.'

'I wish,' remarked a dilapidated skeleton, 'to express my concurrence. When the erection of a monument was contemplated near my place of abode, considerable portions of my anatomy and those of my neighbour got mixed. I have never been quite myself since and the slightest shock now would, I fear, altogether lose for me my individuality. I oppose the present proceedings.'

And so it continued through the night with one objection following another. As dawn approached, a resolution was formulated.

'... to the Members of the Common Council of Saint John we say: - Restez vous la, nor dare to invade the place of our burial.'

And it was unanimously adopted. The resolution was inscribed on the tombstone of a Loyalist who died in 1788 and the meeting dissolved."

Of course, this was the work of some inspired editorial writer at the paper, and not of the ghosts and skeletons of the burial ground.

Nonetheless, the article had the desired effect, for permission for the building of a bandstand in the Old Burial Ground was not granted by the council of the day. However, two years later, just across the street in King's Square, the City Coronet Band erected the present two tiered bandstand in memory of Edward the Seventh. Concerts have been played there ever since, but apparently the music is not objectionable for the rattling skeletons have been quiet ever since that outburst recorded by the "Morning News" scribe in 1906.

The tomb of the Honourable James Putnam (died 1789) might have been the chosen location for the midnight meeting recorded above. It is the most elaborate marker in the burial grounds, and the final resting place of close to a dozen other dignitaries from the Loyalist era, including the first rector of Trinity Church, George Bissett (died 1788) and Jonathan Sewell, (died 1796), who served as the last Attorney General of Massachusetts before the American Revolution.

The Canada Day Ghostly Gallivant sponsored by Market Square has become one of the most popular ways of sharing ghost stories in Saint John. Here, Lynn Adams plays the role of Lady la Tour.

In this Ghostly Gallivant session, Harold Wright shares the story of a trumpeter who lost his life in an accident, but who still plays late at night in the uptown area.

Chapter 12

Haunted Places of Business

Haunted Places of Business

We often hear of haunted houses, and a number of the stories in this book tell of such places, and a few more will follow in the chapter on West Saint John ghosts.

Haunted businesses on the other hand are not so well known. This is not because ghosts are any less likely to be found in such places, but because business hauntings are not as apt to be talked about. After all, business is business, and someday a business might be for sale, and a potential buyer might not want to deal with a ghost as part of the running of his operations. So, if the owner of a business has had an eerie experience or heard a story about a ghostly encounter on the premises, he might not talk about it at all.

This is not an uncommon phenomenon. Business owners, and in fact, many people who have had unexplainable happenings will not reveal their stories lest someone make fun of them. I have met a great many people who have shared stories you will not read in the pages of this book, as they have told the story of a strange encounter with reluctance, and have made me promise it will not be used in any public way. If I did not respect such wishes, I would have a lot of people very upset with me and possibly some of the ghosts they have told me about would take out the anger they feel on me. Fortunately, there are many others who have no problem sharing their stories, though they sometimes ask to remain anonymous. This, of course, is always done when so requested.

Stories do get around about both homes and businesses as you will see in this chapter and the next.

Millidgeville residents along Donaldson Street and Daniel Avenue who dig up their backyards to plant trees are surprised to learn that their house is on one of two runways that served the city when the first major airport was opened in 1929. One runway ran east west, the other runway north and south, and at the north end was the airport's original hanger which served the aircraft for storage and mechanical purposes. Some very tragic events took place on or near the airfield according to historian Harold Wright, who has written a book on the topic of the Millidgeville airport. He shared the following as examples.

"In 1931, a daredevil pilot, Scottie Sterling and his passenger Rudyard Brayley died near the runaway when an outside loop they were tying to execute failed. They crashed near the Royal Kennebecasis Yacht Club. Long distance flyer Ruth Nicholas crash landed the next day. On another occasion, Pilot Jimmy Wade and his passenger K. C. Irving almost lost their lives in a crash not far from the original hanger. During World War Two, the Air Force built a second hanger at what is now 101 Woodward Avenue. Two Air Force Pilots, Alfred B. Jobin and John W. Wood were killed in a crash there on November 11, 1941."

With so many tragedies, there is every reason to believe that the ghosts of some of those involved might still lurk in the area. The employees of Wayside Industries, who took over the Woodward Avenue hanger location and of Coast Tire, who use the former hanger for storage today are certain that ghosts share the space. Over the years, the workers have heard many strange sounds in the old hanger. Certainly some can be attributed to the creaking and groaning that is expected in any old building. However, when workers get a feeling of being watched, and strange footsteps follow them around when they are alone in the old structure, they begin to feel uncomfortable. This feeling is intensified at times when the ephemeral figure of a workman flits in and out of their line of vision. At that point, they are sure there is more going on than winds shifting the building or cold contracting the beams. To date, no one has been able to identify the ghosts, though one man did spend time walking around the vacant building challenging the ghosts to come forth. This sounds like a place for Loyalist City Paranormal to check out!

On Main Street on the city's West Side is Moosehead Breweries, which likes to boast it produces some of Canada's best beer in the country's oldest independent brewery. They do not boast about the ghost that helps in the production, though they do not hide the fact that some of their employees have encountered the ghost from time to time since the firm was established in 1867. In a September 2006 interview, the ghost's ramblings came up in an interview with Derek Oland, then chairman of the board. Oland who is no stranger to ghosts as he lives in a house at New River Beach long known to be haunted, no doubt let the Moosehead ghost story slip out in what was supposed to be a business interview with Chris Morris. The reporter latched on to the idea as the lead into a story about a thirty five million dollar expansion the company was then undergoing in order to remain competitive. According to Morris's version of the story, workers in the very oldest parts of the building, which date back 100 years or more, have had many sightings of a long dead brewmaster hovering over the huge copper vats which have been used for generations in the brewing of the distinctive Moosehead Beer. If this was a singular report, it might be dismissed, but many who have worked in the brewery over the decades have confirmed the sightings and from time to time have added other interesting details to what Morris wrote.

Gordon Miller was a long time engineer and electronics' expert with CFBC radio station, when it operated in one of the oldest uptown buildings at 68 Carleton Street from 1946-1994. It was originally built about 1840 as a wedding present for a member of the Smith family, and was later the home of James F. Robertson of Manchester, Robertson, Allison's huge King Street department store. It then served as the home of the Elk's Club before it was taken over by CFBC in 1946. Among Miller's favorite stories of the building was one about the ghost of its former owner Neil McLean and the tricks he played on "lonely night staff." The ghost, who Miller noted was popularly called the "Senator," by staff who encountered him, because at the time he was a member of the Senate, and also owner of Connor's Brothers fisheries empire in Blacks Harbour. "Therein lies the ghost story," Miller said as he continued the tale saying, "The Senator gave out cans of sardines as Christmas bonuses and what really got people afraid at night is when they smelled sardines," Miller said. "They'd get a whiff of fish coming up the stairs." Miller added that no reason for the scent could be determined, so it was taken that the owner's ghost was around just making sure the guys didn't goof off. "We had people working nights in the building who just took off and never come back," he told reporter Erin Anderssen, (who is now one of the "Globe and Mail's" lead writers) in an interview when the station moved to Chesley Drive in July 1994. In her story, Anderssen playfully wondered if the ghost would move too, but Miller says it did not.

Fragmentary stories exist of ghosts at two uptown establishments in the bed and breakfast businesses. At the Mahogany Manor at 220 Germain St., the former manse of the adjacent Baptist Church, guests report the gauzy figure of a woman carrying a crying baby up the grand central stairway from time to time. It is believed to be the first minister's wife trying to calm a sick child who eventually died. The Manor is still operating, thus, there is the possibility of checking this story out. This can't be done at the former Parker House Inn a few blocks east on the corner of Princess and Sydney, as it is now closed. When operating, it was said to have a ghostly presence that would spin wool on a huge second floor spinning wheel and wake guests at night when at her pre dawn labours.

While some Bed and Breakfasts' would keep such stories quiet, neither of these ones have as the tales are widely known, and the stories did not seem to dissuade guests from enjoying the premises.

In 2010 Ron Sajack painted a mural on the interior walls of the Lancaster Mall, and is shown here working on a depiction of what is now Moosehead Breweries on Main Street West. Another local landmark he included was the Earle House and he playfully included an image of a ghost in the window of that venerable home, though its owner, Margaret Earle, said no ghosts had ever bothered her in the many years she lived there.

Every visiting cruise ship passenger that is driven by this Lancaster Avenue home is told it is a witches house, and haunted. It sure looks it, but when the owner Margaret Earle was living, she was emphatic that she had no trouble with witches or ghosts. The second photo shows the parlour of the home that Margaret enjoyed well into her nineties.

Chapter 13

Meet Some Believers

Meet Some Believers

Make no mistake about it there are many Saint Johners who believe in ghosts, and they have stories to share. Not all the stories they have are detailed enough for a full length chapter, so I thought for this section of the book I would introduce you to a few individuals that have had brief ghostly encounters. Some of these folks did not even realize they were in the presence of a ghost or were having what is called a paranormal experience until after the fact. It was only when they were back home relaxing and recounted a happening that they realized it was a unique unexplainable experience.

Take Valerie Evans who for years regularly ran Murder Mystery presentations and in fact, still does occasionally. When first married, she lived in an apartment on Mecklenburg Street. There was a basement door in the house that was constantly open and Valerie was worried someone might get in through there and create havoc. She asked a neighbour, Barry King to fasten the door solidly, and she thought he had done so, but when he left town, she discovered the door was still open. She thought he must have forgotten to close it, so she figured she better do so herself. She closed the door and hooked it but as soon as she turned to leave, it flew open. She closed the door a second time, taking special care to see that it was hooked. Again the door flew open. She pulled it more firmly into the casing, and made sure it was solidly in the door jamb, and hooked it once again. For the third time, the door flew open when she began to walk away. On her forth attempt to fasten the door it literally shook in her hands as she pulled it closed. Valerie decided the door was determined to stay open, and concluded "if it wants to stay open, then I guess I will leave it open."

At the time she did not think there was a ghostly reason for the door's stubbornness, but upon reflection, that seemed the only possible explanation.

One foggy summer night Jason Watson and a friend were gathering driftwood to keep a fire going for a bit on McLaren's Beach off Sand Cove Road on the West Side. They had left their girlfriends attending the smouldering fire as they scouted the west end of the beach for more wood. As Jason worked his way along the high tide lines, he noted a wispy figure wandering along the water's edge down near the breakwater that lines the beach in front of what was the Inn on the Cove. He wondered how the wispy figure could have gotten down there without his group hearing him on the rattle rock, or seeing him pass by the light of their fire. But there he was, a ragged man who looked like he had just come ashore from a shipwreck. Jason quickly returned to the fire, and at that point his buddy asked him if he had seen the old fellow on the shoreline. The girls piped up, saying they too had seen the man. None of them had any idea where he came from or where he went, for he did not pass them going down to the shore, nor did he pass them returning to the parking lot. Only later did they wonder if it had been a ghost they had seen.

In 1974, three university students were hired to do an inventory of old houses in Saint John. One of the objects was to take interior photographs of some of the buildings. That job was designated to Michael Hiltz, who was assisted by Karen Crandall and Ann Hale in gathering data on the homes. In an interview conducted by John Fogan, an "Evening Times Globe" reporter noted for his down-to-earth and highly accurate accounts,- they told of one house where it proved impossible to get photos as the camera's lighting system failed each time they tried. That house was then owned by Mr. and Mrs. Walter Hoar and was located at 62 Park Street in the Mount Pleasant area of the city. Mr. Hiltz told Fogan that he had no trouble photographing the exterior of the building, which is an imposing limestone structure with a fine widow's walk atop its roof, but inside, he had made three attempts and his lighting equipment failed each time. "The owners," he told Fogan, "had been informed the house was supposed to be haunted." He added that when in Gagetown, he and "members of a CBC crew ran into another alleged ghost who did not like their lighting apparatus," thus, he was convinced that ghosts and haunted houses existed. Despite his encounters, Hiltz told Fogan he was "interested in learning of any other Saint John houses that may be haunted." Fogan ended the piece by asking, "Do you have one?"

If Hogan got any response, it was not carried in subsequent issues of the paper, but, as you know from what you have read, and what you will read in the chapters that follow, there are any number of haunted houses and haunted places in the city of Saint John.

Let us conclude this look at what were considered ghost encounters with the story of a recent sighting on the corner of Tower and Lancaster Streets in Saint John West. A teacher living in the area, Debbie Collicott, was driving from the area of Martello Tower towards the lower west when she spotted a fragmentary figure lurking by a picket fence that had enclosed the former Mayes' mansion that stood on the hilltop for many years.

Debbie said the women turned slightly toward her as she passed by and she could feel the figure's eyes bore through her. She described the woman as being dressed in a long flowing gown that touched the ground, and said she had a shawl about her head. Her immediate thought was that she had encountered Lady La Tour as many other west siders have. However when I related this story to some of my Roman Catholic friends who lived in the area and knew it well, they suggested Debbie had seen, as they had, the ghostly form of a strict nun that had lived in the nearby St. John Street convent and that had taught in the adjacent St. Patrick's School. Many of them said they had had encounters as students with the nun they would rather not recollect and that they had personal experiences with her spirit which still lurked about the area. Who knows?

John Perry, who has lived 96 years in an 1857 house at 290 Tower St, directly east of the corner where the ghostly sightings by Debbie and others have occurred, admits he has never seen the ghost himself, though he's heard many stories about it. "In my mind," he said in a 2012 interview, it all comes from the times long past when Annie Nice used to roam about the area. She was an old lady who lived on St. James Street, and in her later years, wandered the West Side wearing a long tattered dress with a cloak flying from her shoulders. She was harmless, but when I was a boy, we were very frightened of her, especially if she was whisking about at night in Queen Square, or up on the hill over there where the ghost is said to have been spotted so many times."

John's conclusion is one many have reached. They are among those who don't believe, but as this story makes clear, there are just as many who do!

Jason Watson points to where he saw the ghost on McLaren's Beach

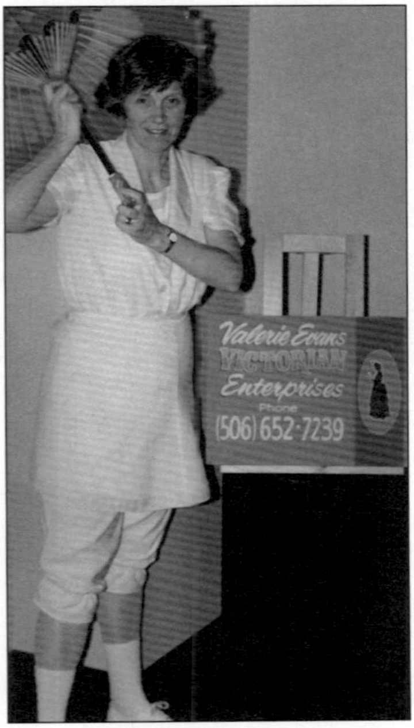

Long time heritage advocate and murder mystery presenter Valerie Evans has lived in many old Saint John homes, and has encountered what she considered a ghost on more than one occasion.

Frances Helyar had quite a scare in Fernhill cemetery when a "Yahoo" came out of the woods. Perhaps it was a similar creature that scared Debbie Collicott on the west side.

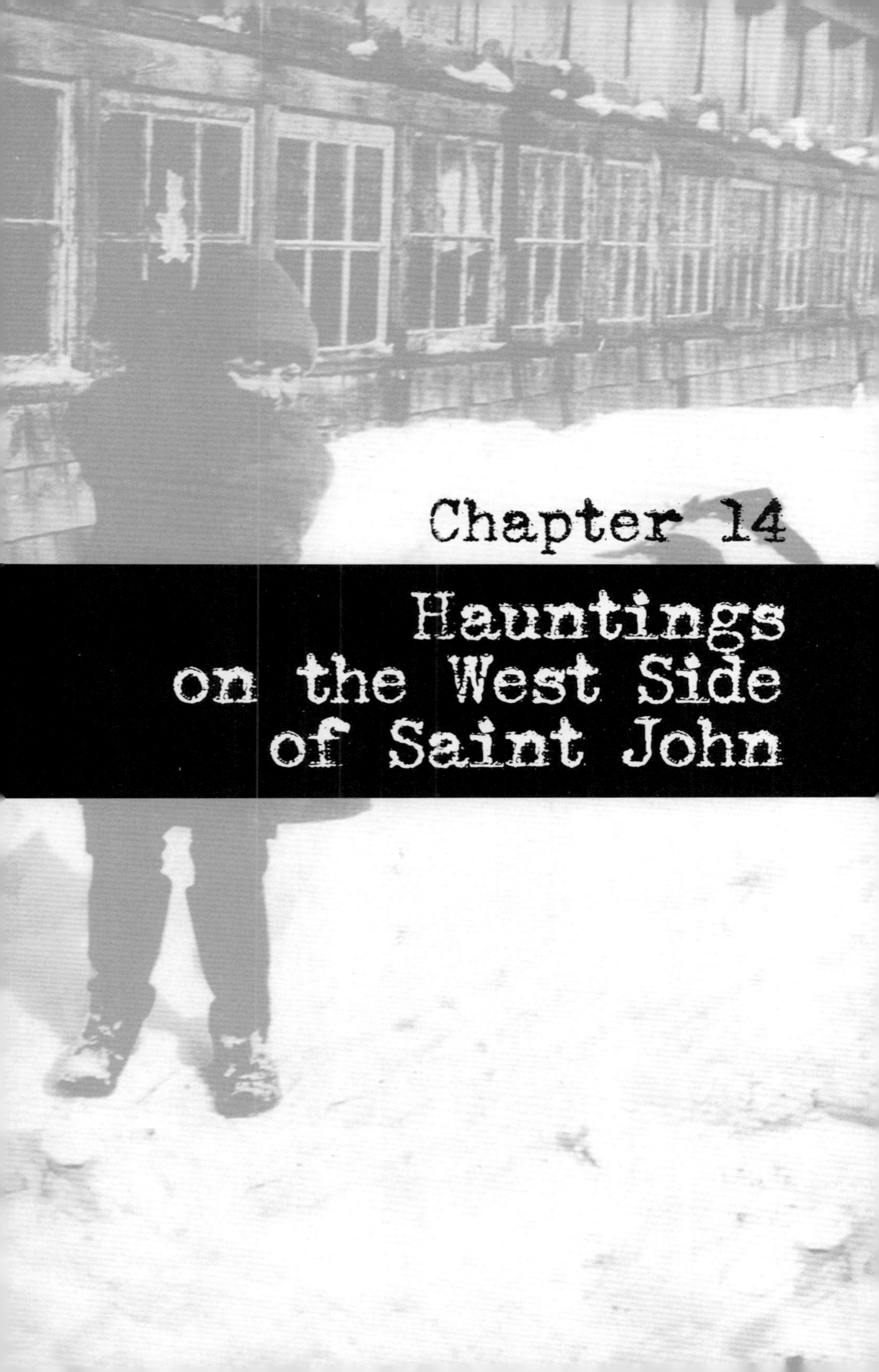

Chapter 14

Hauntings on the West Side of Saint John

Hauntings on the West Side of Saint John

So, now we come to the area of the city that I know best and have been accused of favoring in my career as a writer and Walk n' Talk leader. Well, I can't deny a great attraction for the west side, and having lived in the area all but five of my three score and ten years, I certainly have heard more stories, ghostly and otherwise, in this area of the city west of the river St. John. So, let's get right into it and recount the stories of what seems to me to be the most concentrated area of ghostly encounters in the city, Lancaster Avenue at Duke Street, and just down the hill, the DeMonts Street area.

We start with the latter. DeMonts Street is only a block long and runs north from the highest part of Duke Street to Prince Street. It is known for its fine collection of 1912-1920's era homes built by the Fenton family as one of the earliest suburban developments in the city. We do not think of DeMonts Street as a suburb now, but in the days before cars were common, it was just far enough from the business district of Carleton, as the area below City Line on Saint John West was known, to be considered "out of town." It was a fashionable place to live for those who could afford to move from the flats of the lower west to a self contained house just a bit up the hill.

Among those moving there when the street was first developed was John Berryman Splane. You can see his image on the famous post card of Saint John's King's Square, which is shown here. It was taken as he strolled through King's Square when he lived on King Street East. Splane moved into the house at 458 DeMonts Street in 1915, and lived there until he died in 1972. Then his son John continued to live there and his grandson Michael took over ownership when his father died in 1994.

Michael says he was in the house the night his dad died in the Saint John Hospital and he knew he had passed on even before he got the call. He said that while he was asleep, he felt someone hitting him on the feet to wake him up. When he woke, he knew his dad had died as being tapped on the feet was the way he always woke his son up. Within minutes he got the call from the hospital telling him the bad news.

More strange events were to follow.

When sleeping in his grandfather's bed, Michael would hear someone coming up the steps and then open his bedroom door just a bit. He would have to say, "J.B. it's me Mike," and then the noise would stop and the door would shut.

When Michael married, he and his wife Cindy initially used his grandfather's bed, but when J.B. showed up and cracked the door open a few inches, it frightened his wife so much that the bed was relegated to the attic. When Cindy went to wash up in the bathroom, she often smelled shaving lotion with an aroma her husband didn't use. It was the aroma of "Old Spice" a brand Mike remembered his grandfather preferred.

Cindy says she has been brushed by a presence that has passed her in the pantry and one night, she happened to glance in the kitchen window and saw a face staring back at her. Though she had never met her, she knew it was the image of Mike's mom from pictures she had seen. Their cat, when alive, would sometimes come out of a deep sleep and stand stock still and stare at the hallway as if something was there, but whatever it was, no one else could see it. Their dog did the same.

Through the winter, on cold nights, they would hear shoveling in the basement. Michael said it sounded like coal being scooped up and thrown into the furnace, a sound he recalled from his youth when his helped his granddad shovel the coal in the furnace morning and night to keep the house warm. Of course his granddad, J.B., was long dead, and the old coal furnace had been replaced by oil in the 70's. Yet to this day on cold nights the couple can still hear what sounds like coal being shoveled into the furnace. Nowadays, the regular happenings in the house do not bother either of them, as they have gotten used to the oddities and know there is no threat in having their "granddad" and other deceased members of the family lurking about in the century old house.

Just up the hill from the Splane house, on an embankment at the corner of Lancaster Avenue and Duke Street, Heinrich Biermann was left wondering what was going on in his house too when it was reported a headless lady was seen rocking in the bedroom of his house overlooking the old Beaconsfield Fire Station.

This happened when his son Helmer was a boy in the 1930's, but he didn't share the story till much later.

You see, Helmer was a long time reporter and music critic for the "Telegraph Journal," and was considered a serious man of letters. As such he was also a member of the gentleman's literary group known as the "Fortnightly Club." I was also a member, and on the night November 23, 2004 he shared his ghost story with me.

He said, "A family friend, a gardener named Hans from Glen Falls, came to visit for a few days. We were going to help him celebrate his birthday, but he left immediately after breakfast the morning following his arrival. A neighbour, knowing the guest was slated for a longer visit asked dad why he had left so soon. 'Poor Hans complained that the room he slept in was haunted,' Mr. Biermann senior answered with some annoyance. The neighbour replied, 'He must have seen the old headless lady in the rocking chair'."

"Well, that was quite a shock to dad," Helmer said as he concluded the story. He added, "Up to then, he had no idea we lived with a ghost. From that time on, the room was kept locked and unused as long as we lived there."

As for Hans, Helmer recalled he "visited from time to time, but never came for the night again."

Though the Biermanns did not know of the ghost, it seems it was common knowledge in the community. Recently, I joined Don Schell for a west side tour where he recollected his youth there in the 1930's. When we passed a set of cement steps leading up the embankment where the Biermann's house stood, Don noted "those steps led to a haunted house, and we never went near that place." Though I believed Helmer Biermann's story when he told it, it was great to have Don's confirmation.

Two other ghosts also are known to be active, or were known to be active in this vicinity. At Tilton's Corner, there was the Shade of Jewett, and that story is told in greater detail in the chapter titled, "Where do ghosts go when they go?" But I note it here because of its proximity to the other two. At Hillcrest Church, the caretaker had a problem with lights coming on at night when he was trying to rest up at home. Members of the congregation would call him saying they drove by and he'd left lights on, but he knew he hadn't. Eventually, the problem resolved itself, but why it happened was never discovered. Also at that church, Jason Watson, who you'll recall from the McLaren's Beach tale in the last chapter, was on volunteer security duty one night as there was a sleep over, and they were concerned the girls might be bothered by teenage boys who knew they were there. On checking the parking lot, sure enough, someone was spotted in the fringe of woods that separate the parking lot from the adjacent graveyard. Jason and the other males went out to check it out. A shadowy figure came out of the woods, flew- yes, that's the right word, flew across the parking lot, and disappeared between two huge houses at the south of the lot. The men gave chase, and when they reached Buena Vista Avenue looked west, and saw the still flying figure entering the graveyard. By the time they got to the gate, nothing could be seen. There were no more sightings, nor have there been any since, but it is something Jason will never forget.

While not in this immediate area, there are two other stories that happened only a few blocks away that fit nicely into this section of stories on what was formerly called Beaconsfield and Carleton.

On the corner of Watson and Guilford stands the former home of Dr. M.H. Peters. Its fine architectural features including gothic doors and windows, elaborate gingerbread trim, and rooftop finials that catch the eye, giving it the appearance of a house that has a story to tell. Indeed it has a rich history. Peters was the resident Saint John West doctor when ether was first used as an anesthetic in Canada in his Guilford Street home in January 1847. He was a commissioner of the Water Board when water was first piped to Carleton in 1859 and in charge of the troops on Carleton Heights as Lt. Col. during the Fenian threat in the mid 1860's. Peter's lost his life as a result of a wound to the head when he was hit by a brick while fighting a fire at John K. Taylor's Carleton home in January 1887. Whether this unexpected death has anything to do with the ongoing haunting of his old house is unknown, but what is known is that a ghost or ghosts have manifested themselves on many occasions in the house since his death. When Foster Hammond owned the house, he openly talked about the ghosts to anyone who dropped by. One night, I did just that during a Walk n' Talk. I was sharing the above little known details about Peters and Hammond, hearing us outside, wondered what was going on. He came to his doorway and when I asked if the house was haunted, he told the crowd that his children had seen the ghost on many occasions, that the dogs and cats follow the ghost around the house, that the ghost moves things around inside the house, and the ghost plays the piano at night. He recalled one occasion that spontaneous piano music floated through the house. He said his wife believed it was the cat doing the tinkling of the ivories, until the cat was found to be curled up and asleep. On another night, some visitors to a party saw a lady in a long black dress with her hair in a bun quietly circulating through the crowd, but when they enquired among themselves about her identity, no one knew who she was. Hammond said that guests enjoy parties at his home, but will not stay overnight as they say they feel a presence in the house that makes them uncomfortable. Finally, he said, his aged mother had an apartment in the attic area, and though she prohibited him from allowing people in to clean the place, she was constantly berating him for letting cleaners in, when he had not done so at all. She claimed to see them, and would chase them off as she wanted her apartment left as it was.

"We don't feel it's a harmful presence, or mean spirited," Foster concluded that August day in 2006. He sold the house after his mom died, not because of the ghost, but because he had retired, and the care of a rambling old house had become too much work for him.

Just a block south from the Peter's House is the former home of the well known Saint John artist Miller Brittain. For years, his paintings hung in the house while his mother and sister lived there, but though none hang there today, there is at least one person who believes that the ghost of Miller Brittain is still hanging around.

Georgina Stafford shared the story on August 27th 2008 after hearing unexplained knockings in the house when babysitting there. These noises occurred each afternoon around 2 o'clock. One of the children kept seeing a figure on the stairs leading from the kitchen to the back of the house. Another figure appeared on the stairs at the front of the house and the child claimed to have talked to the individual. Then there was an appearance in the downstairs dining room, and when Georgina entered, she found her clothes became very cold, as did the two young children, yet, another girl sitting in the room was warm as toast.

Georgina was left wondering what was going on, but it didn't scare her off- she still goes to the house awaiting further adventures with what might be Miller Brittain's ghost.

Just up the hill from these sites stands the oldest church in the city, St. George's, in operation continuously since 1821. It's the sort of place where you would expect to encounter ghosts, but there are no genuine ghost tales to be told. However, there is one story that is well known and it was invented by Frank Etwell in the 80's when he was a Cub Leader at the church. During a sleep over, the boys would not settle down so Frank told them he was going to call forth all those who had died in the past year to quiet them down. He told the boys that at midnight, the recent dead came walking out of the door of the tower. At the tower clock stuck twelve, the boys experienced a fierce and lengthy rattling of the tower door, which, of course, Frank had arranged. That did the trick and that incident led to the story of ghost of the tower of St. George's that is told to this day as a genuine ghost happening.

Knowing that some tales you hear have an explanation, it does leave one wondering what one would find if one could get to the origin of many of the other tales that have been recounted and which will follow.

J.B. Splane as he appeared on a Saint John Postcard prior to moving to DeMonts Street.

Helmer Biermann as a youngster stands beside the chicken coop outside the house where Hans saw the headless lady in his room. Photo Credit Helmer Biermann

Foster Hammond shares the stories of many ghostly encounters he experienced when he owned Peter's House, corner of Watson and Guilford Street, Saint John West.

Chapter 15

Centracare Had Its Share of Ghosts

Centracare Had Its Share of Ghosts

Though it is a half kilometer from the Lancaster Avenue, Duke Street, DeMonts street area, Centracare was close enough to these areas that it should be considered as having been part of the most concentrated ghost area of Saint John.

During its time, it was known as Canada's oldest asylum for those with mental health disorders and stood brooding over the gushing river at the Reversing Falls in Saint John from 1848 until it closed in 1998. For all of its 150 years, the work of the institution was carried on compassionately by the medical staff, the nurses, the attendants, and many patients were able to return to the work-a-day world and the home environment due to the treatment received in the institution.

Yet, it was never easy for the hospital to attract staff to work at Centracare nor to convince the general public it was a place to visit those being cared for. Not only was Centracare a foreboding cluster of very Victorian buildings that stretched over the four acres of hilltop property, there was also the stigma of mental illness itself. Many families would hide a sufferer away rather than admit that one of the family members was in need of help.

These situations gave rise to many stories of strange occurrences in and around the institution that kept those without business at the hospital away from its doors.

Many of the stories involve the treatments patients received. Some treatments were on the leading edge of mental health practice and good results were realized. Sadly, the outcome of other treatments was not so good. In the quest for cures, many strange theories were tried out in the Saint John institution that did not work for the benefit of the patient.

It seemed the stories that circulated most readily were those told when something went wrong, and those about what were taken as hauntings at the hospital.

None of the "ghostly" occurrences so readily spoken of have ever been proven authentic, yet they persisted among the staff while the building stood and are still told to this day by those who worked in and around the Centracare facility.

The story most often told is of a man wearing a dark cape and a black top hat who when seen at the institution was considered to be a premonition of death. It was always said the man was Dr. Waddell, the first of the medical directors who served the hospital from 1848-1875.In most tellings of the tale, it is said that Waddell comes to certify that a patient has died, making him somewhat of a phantom coroner. Not all think of this phantom figure as Dr. Waddell as some believe it is a phantom undertaker from a nearby funeral home.

What is the basis for those who favour the belief the figure is Dr Waddell? Well, he lived in a third floor apartment in the asylum and often did his rounds at night. He knew the building intimately and at times would seemingly appear out of nowhere to study a ward to be sure he was getting an accurate idea of what was going on. He oversaw the building of major additions in the 1860's and he knew all the intricate attic passageways that connected the buildings. Thus, he could appear anywhere in the institution unannounced, and probably did so from time to time just prior to a death occurring, thus the origin of the tale, which was widely known among the staff until the institution closed.

In his day, Dr. Waddell was seen from time to time gazing toward the city while standing under a huge elm on the embankment that overlooks the Reversing Falls. At that time the slope to the falls was the location of the institution's farm, and Dr. Waddell no doubt visited the gardens and pasture land on a regular basis to ensure that the animals were treated well, and the crops were being harvested properly. Long after the gardens were moved to Sand Cove Road, and Waddell had died, what was taken as his ghost would be seen in long tails and high hat standing under a huge elm and staring out over the Reversing Falls. Out of such sightings grew the belief that the first resident doctor, though long dead, never left his post and if his image was seen, it was the belief that a death would occur in the institution that very day.

As the hospital grew from 200 to 1700 beds, a half kilometer or more of tunnels were built linking the various buildings. In the attics, catwalks existed that those in the know could use for passing between buildings. Strange shapes were sometimes seen, and other times strange noises were heard in the attic areas of the hospital. These sightings and sounds were often connected with the death of a patient, which, with a great number of elderly people, occurred almost daily.

One story is told of a mother who was dying in far off northern New Brunswick who supposedly came for a final visit to her hospitalized daughter. The asylum patient was convinced her mom had actually visited. The officials were almost ready to believe it had somehow happened as the patient claimed until they found out the mother had died in a far off county. What was most eerie about the case was that the mother's death occurred at the exact time her daughter claimed she had visited her, yet that patient had no way of knowing her mother had died or knowing when she had died.

Another story involves a confused patient who was lost in the tunnels. A guard on duty, in a state of semi-sleep after many hours of inactivity, was startled awake by the wispy figure of a lady swooping along the tunnels at one of their many intersections. The ghostly figure started down one of the branches that had no exit. At that point the guard stirred from his station, and followed the lady into the tunnel. It became darker and darker and then she just disappeared. He searched several hiding places, tried doorways to abandoned treatment rooms, but found each door locked, and eventually had to call for backup. His colleagues arrived with flashlights, but there was no one to be found. A check of rooms determined no patients missing yet the guard knew he had been awakened and passed by a woman that glided along the passageway that night. There was never an explanation for this event, but similar sightings continued to plague guards over the decades.

Improvements to the hospital were continuous over the years. When a central switchboard was installed in the fifties with a board that lit up whenever any phone was used in any of the rooms, it led to an interesting situation. One night, a light flashed showing a phone in use in a room that was known to be vacant, so a guard was dispatched to see what was going on. The room was locked as it should have been, but when he entered the phone was definitely off the hook. He replaced it and the light went out. A short time passed and he was asked once again to check the room as the switchboard once again showed a phone in use. The room was still locked, but the phone was definitely removed from the hook and lying on the night table. Again the phone was replaced, and the guard felt a bit spooked, but there was nothing he could see that explained why the phone was removed, nor was there any sign that anyone had been in the room, or was still hidden there.

The guard went back to work. The problem continued for several days, and there was never any explanation. The room was watched carefully, and there was no one entering or leaving. The room remained unoccupied, yet the switchboard kept lighting up, and the phone would be found off the hook.

The guard got so spooked, he would not longer answer night time calls to make checks. So, maintenance staff was called, and they surmised that traffic rumbling by on Bridge Road to the north of the institution was jarring the phone enough to knock it off the hook. Perhaps it was a good explanation, but it leaves a question. As traffic on this road is 24/7 there really was no way to explain what was happening to the phone in that one room wasn't also happening in any nearby rooms.

There may be logical explanations for all of the incidents mentioned, and others that could be told, but they will remain unsolved as the buildings that housed Canada's oldest mental hospital are now but a memory.

Credit for these stories must be given to Joe Hunt who shared them while I was doing a book for Mind Care called, "150 years of Caring, the continuing history of Canada's Oldest Mental Health Facility." The book contains the stories of American mental health agitator Dorothea Dix's visit to what became Centracare in 1872; Houdini's supposed visit to the hospital in 1896 and a tragic double axe murder that occurred just 6 years after the institution opened. This alone must have caused some doubt as to whether institutionalization was the right direction to go with mental health patients.

From 1848, and for 150 years, this very Victorian era cluster of building variously known as the Lunatic Asylum, the Provincial Hospital, and lastly Centracare, served to treat the mentally ill of New Brunswick at the site overlooking the Reversing Falls in Saint John West.

This photo provides a glimpse into one of the many tunnels that connected various buildings in the sprawling mental health complex. Though the buildings were torn down in 1999, perhaps the tunnels still exist under the grassy park known as Wolastoq.

Chapter 16

The Ghost of Black Charlie's Hill in Milford

The Ghost of Black Charlie's Hill in Milford

This is a story told in the Randolph- Milford area of Saint John's west side, which became a convenient place to live because it was within walkable distance of a number of local employers. Milford is found on both sides of a promontory that squeezes the St John River at the Pokiok Narrows, and overlooks the St.John River just above the Reversing Falls.

Many lived there because they could walk into Fairville to jobs at the Simm's Broom and Brush Factory, which just closed in 2013. At one time it was Canada's largest manufacturer of brooms, brushes, rollers, etc. and most ladies living near the huge factory got their first jobs right out of school working on the assembly lines. Many of the ladies' male companions worked just a block up the street from Simm's at Moosehead Breweries, or just east of Moosehead where the Canadian Pacific Railway had its station and rail yard. Some worked at both of these concerns, as Moosehead needed more men in summer than winter to produce beer, and the railway needed more men in winter than summer to clean tracks and move winter port freight.

Thus, the communities of Randolph and Milford became convenient places for these workers to live and they built simple but strong homes in the area.

A hundred years ago, there were also saw and lumber mills and limestone quarries in this area that provided work. Up to the 40's Dwyer's huge bakery provided jobs for upwards of 100 baking staff, and when the sawmills and quarries and the bakery folded up the men and women who lost their jobs could still find work about a kilometer or two away at the Provincial

Hospital, or the Partington (now Irving) Pulp mill.

The folks living in this area loved the country like atmosphere, where they could garden, fish, and enjoying swimming at nearby Dominion Park in summer, and skating on the St. John River in winter.

Among the many attractive places in Randolph and Milford for a stroll on Sunday afternoon was a knoll of land that rose out of the river just above the Reversing Falls that was known as Black Charlie's Hill. Though no one knows for sure, it is assumed a black family once lived in the area, thus its name. No one lives there today, but that doesn't mean the area does not have its stories.

One story came to light on a Walk n' Talk I was leading in Saint John West one night a few years ago. This is how it went:

"Ever hear the story of the ghost of Black Charlie's Hill in Milford, Dave?" asked my cousin Ian's granddaughter, Alison Goss as we were puffing up a steep Saint John West hill on a ghost tour. "No, tell me," I said between gulps for air.

"Well there was this rich sea captain named Johann Smith and he had a home in Milford, but he was away a lot at sea, and was leaving his wife alone a lot. She didn't like it much, so she got herself a boyfriend," she began.

Her father Chris, walking beside her in the dark, piped up. "This was in the early 1800's, when men could be away for months and months, but one night, the Captain showed up, and surprised his wife and her boyfriend."

"He killed the man," Alison said, "and his wife ran out of the house, and started to run toward the hill and river. The captain chased her, and when she came to the edge of Black Charlie's Hill, she ran right off the cliff and fell to her death into the river."

Chris and Alison knew the story because of my cousin Ian, their father and grandfather respectively.

"Gramp was driving a taxi down the Milford Road one night and had just passed the Milford School when he was startled to see the forms of two persons come chasing across the road," Alison said. " First a lady in long old time clothes came running out of the hill beside the school and just behind her, came the figure of an old sea captain, chasing her."

"Dad stopped the car," Chris continued, "and watched as they disappeared into the scrub alder of the hill overlooking the river."

Alison continued. "Gramp went back to the taxi office, and he told the other drivers what he had seen, and they told him it was Johann Smith's ghost chasing his wife over the cliff of Black Charlie's Hill."

Knowing Ian as I did, he was probably a bit freaked out by what he was told, but once he settled down, he probably tried to find out what he could about what he'd seen.

Unfortunately, that was not much as I found out when I tried to follow up on the story.

The first one I asked was long time Milford Road resident Pauline Magee and she did not know of the story. "Only thing I can tell you," she said, "is that it's Black Charlie's Hill as the kids burnt it every year and it sure made for good blueberry picking, but we never saw a ghost there."

Then I queried Marilyn Upton who I hoped might be able to help but neither she nor her mother had heard the story though they lived on the side of the Black Charlie's Hill for decades.

"If anyone can verify your story" Marilyn told me, "it would be Donnie Coholan, who lives at the top of the hill."

So, I visited Donnie and he said, "Oh, we knew there was a ghost there, all right," Donnie laughed when I finally got him away from the extensive garden he's developed around the outcropping opposite Black Charlie's Hill.

"Yes, indeed," he said, "mother always warned us to stay off the hill, especially at night, as there was a ghost there, but she never told us who the ghost was, or how it came to be there. I wish I could help you, Dave," he said, "but she never told us the full story....just knowing there was a ghost was enough, I guess."

One that was supposed to know the story was Donnie's uncle, Lou Murphy, but in the three books he wrote that included Milford stories, it is not mentioned.

"That doesn't mean it didn't happen, though," Donnie said. "Lou didn't write all his stories down."

That's where this story might have ended if I hadn't received a second call from Pauline McGee. Excitedly she said, "Give Dot Purdy a call, David, she knows the story behind the ghost."

And so I called Dot and she told me what she thinks my cousin saw that foggy night in Milford, and, in her opinion, it was not a ghost. She said, "That was old Mrs. McMillan. She had lost it in the last of her life and she used to wander around the hills here. Some claim she seemed to be floating off the ground, and she would glide across the road by the school with her arms extended in front her and walk into the woods at Black Charlie's. Mrs. Coyle lived right across the street, and she used to tell the story, and I think that's the way the legend of the ghost began."

And it may be.....but since we can't ask Ian, I prefer the story he told his son and which he and his grand daughter shared with me one June night when we were walking about and talking of the many ghosts of Saint John.

Lou Murphy was as knowledgeable as any one who ever lived in Milford, and, though he did several books in which he could have mentioned the Ghost of Black Charlie's Hill, he did not do so.

Send a Ghost Story to the Author

This is your chance to send your Saint John story to the author and you will, in return, receive a Halloween Haunted House to help you decorate next time the scary season comes along.

Send your story to David Goss, 21 Glenwood Drive, Saint John, E2M 5P3, or via e mail to gosswalk@nbnet.nb.ca. Who knows, it might be in the next book I put together.

The prize is pictured, but since each one turns out differently, it might vary from this photo.

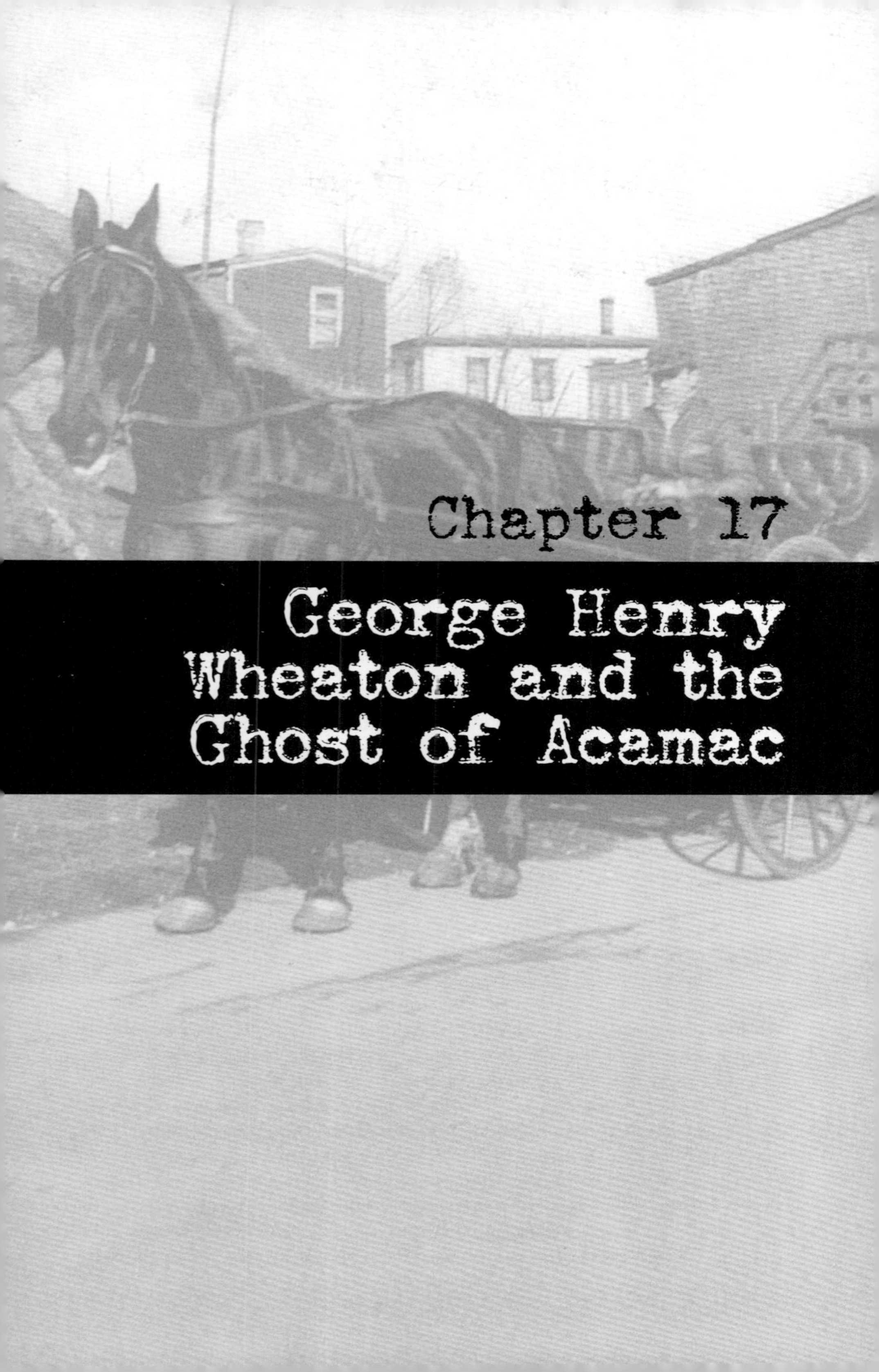

Chapter 17

George Henry Wheaton and the Ghost of Acamac

George Henry Wheaton and the Ghost of Acamac

In the last decade of his long life, I was privileged to meet several times with George Henry Wheaton of Clarendon. On a number of occasions he shared the story of his family, and how they came to live in the area, the work they did, and his own career with the Canadian Pacific Railway, from which he drew his first check in 1926, and for which he had worked until retirement.

George had many amazing stories to tell; some were of his own exploits, and others were of things that happened before he was born and were shared with him by his parents and siblings.

The story of the Ghost of Acamac is among the latter. George shared the story with me at his home on March 23, 1992.

Acamac today is part of the City of Saint John, thus this story fits into this collection, but when this story occurred, Acamac, though it had a sawmill and a quarrying operation was primarily a summer colony. It became attractive to city dwellers after the rail service began in 1889, as they could easily catch a train to and from Fairville and travel to Acamac and points beyond like Martinon, Grand Bay-Westfield, Sagwa, etc. to enjoy their summers in simple cottages by the St. John and Nerepis Rivers.

Some of these cottages were converted to year round dwellings relatively early in the last century and in this case, a junkman from the city had bought a rough cottage property to which he moved his very pregnant wife to live as it was cheaper than living in town. Now this junkman had a problem with the bottle, and he often went to town, supposedly on business, but in reality to engage in several day long drinking bouts and the poor wife would be left alone for long periods.

As she came nearer to delivery time, she became ill, and he left for the city saying he would get a doctor and be back quickly. Again, drink came first, and he did not return, and the baby and mother died in the cottage due to complications during the birth. When he returned, he knew he had done wrong, and he decided to hide the evidence. He cut up the body and loaded it on his peddler's wagon and disposed of it here and there over the next while as he picked up junk, rags, and other items of his trade. He told anyone who asked about his wife that she had gone upriver so her sister could assist with delivery of their child.

Years later when George Henry Wheaton's family came from Harcourt, Kent County, to live in Grand Bay, King's County, they were offered the peddler's cabin at Acamac, and were glad to have a roof over their heads. They weren't told that anyone who had tried to live in the cottage could not stand the place due to visits from the ghost of the peddler's wife to her former cottage and the eerie rattle of the peddler's wagon that seemed to circle the driveway outside the house, but was never actually seen by anyone in the house.

As George related it to me the family learned of the ghost when his older brother, Havelock, came to visit his parent's cottage one night. He said, "Havelock had grown some and was staying out with other people. He came home one night and everyone was in bed, and there was no where for him to sleep except on the couch in the dining room. He lay down on the couch and went to sleep. Some time during the night Havelock woke up to see what he thought was mother coming out of the washroom with a basket of clothes. He watched her come out through the kitchen and go right out the back door into the woodshed. She continued through the woodshed door to the porch where she began to hang the clothes out. He watched her hanging the clothes even though it was the middle of the night. He thought it was strange but eventually fell back to sleep. In the morning when they were having breakfast he said to mother, 'Why were you hanging clothes in the middle of the night?' Mother looked at him surprised and said, 'I wasn't hanging clothes out last night.' She went out to look and sure enough the basket of clothes she had planned to hang out in the morning was gone and she went out and sure enough the clothes were all on the line, the basket leaning against the wall in the woodshed. They couldn't understand how that could happen. They worried about it for a while but they never took it too seriously. They were there for a year and heard all kinds of strange noises and things happened that bothered them tremendously at the time, but they never paid too much attention to it."

He continued, "One day when dad came in from the woods, he and mother were having lunch at the table before they went to bed and as they were talking, having cake and tea, they heard a wagon coming up the road through a little bit of snow on the ground. They heard it rattle right up to the door and stop. Dad got up and got a chair from the dining room for whoever it was, as they expected a knock on the door, and soon the person would be invited to join them in their lunch. They waited for the knock at the door, but no knock came. Mother got up to look out the door. There was no one in the yard. There were wagon tracks and horse shoe prints which stopped outside the door, but they didn't turn around and they didn't leave the yard. They just stopped, and it appeared the wagon had gone straight up into the air and disappeared.

They looked the situation over and they wondered if they had been hearing things, though the tracks were there. They worried about it for a while and then got it out of their system. Two or three more things gave them a start. They lived in that house for two years and heard many things they could not account for."

After two years the family moved upriver and one night a man came knocking at their door, and asked if he could talk to them in confidence about the time they had lived in the cottage at Ketepec. This is the way George recounted that meeting.

"Dad invited the man in and told him he had lived in the house for two years. The man then asked father if he had seen or heard anything that would cause him to wonder what the situation was. My father started to tell him of some of his experiences, when the man said, 'I've heard enough! I've heard enough! We've been living there for six months and we are moving out because we can't stand some of the things that are going on around the house. We can find no reason for it, we can't stand it, and so we are moving out'. "

This aroused his parent's curiosity, George noted, and he concluded the story by saying that they began to inquire why strange things were happening around that house and that is when they were told the story of the junk dealer and his poor pregnant wife's demise.

George said that his parents concluded that the woman hanging out the clothes in the night was the ragpicker's wife, still trying to carry on her wifely duties and that the wagon they heard coming up to the door was the ragpicker himself coming to do away with the remains of his wife and their child. George's parents knew no way of stopping such happenings, nor did all those who tried to live in the cottage over the years it would seem.

As far as George knew, at the time of the sharing of the story, the cottage still stood near the rail tracks at the Ketepec Station. Thus, to this day, the cottage's occupants may be awakened at night by sounds and sights they cannot account for.

It would be a wagon like the one pictured here that the rag picker might have used in going about the upriver countryside- and perhaps, as George believed, he continued to do so long after his death as a phantom peddler.

Among the first to offer ghost tours in Saint John was Joan Pearce, whose brother Rick Peacock played the role of grave stone carver in one of these summer walks of yesteryear in the old Burial Ground.

Chapter 18

River Valley Railroad Ghost

River Valley Railroad Ghost

In the summer of 2013 as part of a Walk n' Talk series I included a hike in the Acamac-Belmont cottage community that has become a year round suburban enclave today. Many residents who live there have no idea of its background, where its name came from, what industries flourished there, how the KBM came to be, or who lived there in the past. For example, one of the highlights was a visit to the cottage where Donald Sutherland summered and was known to have presented skits and plays long before he became famous.

Another was the story of a ghost that troubled residents of the area 80 years ago. To tell the story, like Sutherland, I wrote a skit about the supposed backland ghost that hunted the railway cuts to the west of the Belmont area. It is based on an account that first appeared in the September 15, 1933 Evening Times Globe and which was written by one U.V.Caulfield.

Since we could not locate the writer or any descendants that could tell us any more than the story related, we do not know what his story was based on. To share it, I asked two local actors, David Cook and Willow Edwards, to take on the roles of a courting couple circa 1920, and they were having a telephone conversation from her cottage in Belmont to his home in Grand Bay, a distance of five kilometers or so apart. I acted as the narrator. This is what the Walk n' Talk participants heard.

Narrator-

In the early years of the past century, most of the people living in this area were summer only residents, but there were a few year round residents who had both power and lights from the old Musquash dam that began operations in the early 20's. Such were the families of this couple that we have here, the gentleman living in Grand Bay, and his lady friend in Belmont. About the only way for them to get together was by walking from one point to the other. Usually, this was done on the weekend, often after church on Sunday when there would be a time for long walks. If both families had phones, they could talk, but as you know, it is a lot more interesting to meet than to talk. One night, about nine o'clock David, in Grand Bay, called his sweetie, Willow in Belmont:

The phone rings. Willow picks it up.

David: Willow, I just have to see you tonight. I can't wait till Sunday, I miss you so much. I just want to hug you and kiss you……

Willow: David, stop that mushy talk, you know this is a party line and there might be a half dozen people listening in on this conversation. Anyway, it is already 9 o'clock. You know dad will not let me stay out past 11. Even if you left right now, you wouldn't get here till 10. That would only leave us an hour. Dad might not even let me go out in the dark.

David: Willow, I just have to come down. Even if we only have an hour, that will be better than not seeing you till Sunday. I'll take the shortcut and follow the tracks down. That will get me there in half an hour if I hustle.

Willow: Ohhh! David…not the tracks, never take the tracks, especially at night. You know that area is haunted. Something so bad happened there, that people will not even say what it was, but they do say it's haunted and that no one has ever got through there at night. Don't try that David.

David: Phooey, Willow, those are just stories. I've heard them all, and you know it all started back when they laid those tracks through the rock behind Belmont. That was 30 or 40 years ago. There was a shanty town down your way where the men lived. They were a tough breed of men, they worked hard, they drank too much, and they got lonely for the company of women. They didn't want the locals coming around disturbing their parties, so they made up a story about one of the ladies who took a walk one night and there was a rock slide and she ended up being buried under the rubble beside the tracks. They say you can hear the rocks fall to this day, and hear her cry for help. But I don't believe a word of it. Can I come down?

Willow: Well, David, I don't think you should take the chance to come by the tracks, and if you come by the road, you won't get here till after ten, and even then, dad would not welcome you here at that hour, so you better not come.

David: I'm coming, Willow. Nothing is going to keep me from seeing you. Watch for me, and sneak out of the house if you have to.

Willow: Why don't you wait till tomorrow night, David?

David: I've got to work at the mill tomorrow, Willow. They just got a load of logs to cut and I'll be plumb worn out tomorrow. I'm coming tonight, Willow, watch for me.

Willow: Oh, what will I do....Dad will kill me if I get caught sneaking out to see David...but I really want to see him too....What will I do?

Narrator: It is now 10:00 p.m.

Willow: Well, if David took the short cut he should be here by now, but I don't see him. Perhaps he stayed on the road...he'll be along by 10:30 if he did. Oh, I hope dad has gone to bed and is asleep by then.

Narrator: It is now 10:30 p.m.

Willow: I don't see any sign of David out there. I wonder what could have happened to him. I think I heard dad go out. I wonder what he is doing out there. I wonder if he heard me talking to David and is going to meet up with him and keep him away from the house. Ohm! It is getting later.

Narrator: It is now 11:00 p.m.

Willow: I'm so tired, and still no sign of David. I can't imagine what happened to him. I'm so worried...and so sleepy....I hope he took the road and got tired of walking and went back home. I'll watch for a bit more, but I think I am going to fall asleep soon.

Narrator: It is now 11:30 p.m.

The phone rings and Willow grabs it.

David: Willow.... Willow.....

Willow: Hello! Hello! Is that you David? It doesn't sound like you at all.

David: It's me Willow. I thought you'd be worried so, I thought I better call you.

Willow: David, you sound terrible. Where are you? What happened?

David: I took the tracks, Willow, just as I told you. Boy, I will never do that again. Those are not just stories about it being haunted. It is haunted! The first mile or so, all was quiet, and then it got so dark, and so quiet, I began to get nervous and the hair was standing up on the back of my neck. I was sweating like a pig. I thought I was getting close to your place and soon I would be at your door, when all of a sudden I hear the most terrible clattering and clashing, and it seemed like the ground was opening up under me and was going to swallow me whole. Then I heard the most awful moaning and cries for help. That was it for me. I turned tail and I ran back to my house as fast as I could. The whole time I was running, I swear something was right behind me breathing down my neck. I won't be taking those tracks again. Guess I won't be seeing you till Sunday.

Willow: Well, David, try to calm down and get some sleep. You have a long day at the mill tomorrow. You need your rest. So do I, I guess. Dad has just come in, so I have to get off the phone. He's saying he's got some kind of story to tell me about some guy he just spooked up at the tracks. I'll tell you all about it tomorrow. Goodnight darling.

So ended the story. Everyone realized that, that particular night, it was not a ghost that kept David and Willow apart, but her dad.

However, having shared the story in that way, let me assure you, dear reader that in the Caulfield version, there is not, in any way, an allusion to the fact that it was Willow's dad that scared David off. No, sir, Caulfield gives the story straight, telling of one lad from Grand Bay who dared take the tracks one night, rather than the "tortuous and round about road to get by the haunted cut." He shared how the lad was surprised by the "darkness of the area," and how he heard such a "clattering and clashing he thought the whole side of he cut was opening up to swallow him." So, in retelling it, I just put these words into David's mouth.

Caulfield concluded his tale by saying, "Thereafter, the area was avoided."

And as far as we know, it should still be avoided to this day.

David Cook and Willow Edwards are thespian enthusiasts who are always willing to share ghost stories by dressing the part and playing the roles of those long dead.

Chapter 19

Ghosts and the Union Club

Ghosts and the Union Club

Ghosts are often said to come back from the other side in order to settle some unfinished business, or deal with a grievance or problem left over from the days when they were living. Thus, the longer a home stands, the better the chance someone will have a reason to return to it after they are officially departed.

One of the places that this is reported as happening is at the Union Club which has stood on the Corner of Princess and Germain since 1890 and has been the scene of many social gatherings over the decades. It began life as a retreat strictly for gentleman in the tradition of the English clubs it emulates and therein might lay the problem, for, despite the reluctance and protests of some males, the club has had lady members for almost a century now.

The club has had ghosts for all those years, too, according to some of the long time members of the club, and this belief is especially strong among the staff that serve the needs of the members and are on the premises before and after the social occasions for which the club is justly famed.

In this account, no names will be used because it might embarrass those who shared the stories, but anyone who doubts the accuracy of what follows should be sure to make a visit to the facility and linger a bit after most everyone has gone to see if the experiences of some of the serving staff is repeated when the building is mostly vacant.

In speaking with staff over the years, the stories they have told have been consistent. Some staff say there's nothing at all unusual about the place; that anything that seemed unusual, even ghostly in nature was typical of old house happenings....windows that fly open, doors that would not stay shut, cupboards that open without assistance, blinds that do not stay down when placed down or up when rolled up. Such things, they claim, are easily explained as mechanical aberrations.

But when such things happen regularly or if some other strange phenomenon is noticed, some staff members come to the conclusion that there might be something beyond the range of normal happening. Thus, if a door or window unaccountably flies open and a room suddenly cools off, and it seems as if something or someone has walked into the room, then it might not just be a draft....it could be something more sinister.

In a building as old as the Union Club, and one heated by steam, there is bound to be a fair amount of hissing, cracking, and snapping as the building cools at night. But when it is accompanied by voices, and there are no humans left on the premises to make such sounds, then person's hearing those voices in a supposedly vacant building start to wonder if there is something or someone still in the building with them. And when they do not find anyone, they are left to wonder just what it was they heard.

Over the years, many staff have heard strange voices in the basement, and having become certain that someone had gone down there to use the washrooms, and was perhaps experiencing a problem, had gone down to the rescue. But, to their surprise, not a soul was found to be there. So, what did they hear?

Some would say the plumbing was acting up; others would say the wind was whistling around the walls, and others might attribute the sound to revelers passing by on the street heading to the bars just down the hill. All very plausible explanations but not always the case it would seem.

Take, for instance the staff member finishing the dish cleanup who distinctly heard guttural voices as the last of the dishwater drained from the sink. The voice was coming up the drainpipe and seemed to be calling for help. Convinced there might be someone downstairs in the washroom, a check was made but not a soul was in the basement, or anywhere else in the building. The staff member involved recalled feeling a chill run up her back when the sounds continued to occur, and she soon exited the building.

Later, she spoke to others about the sounds and found that many, when supposedly alone in the building, had heard what they took to be the sound of men in conversation in the parlour, or around the bar. Upon investigation, however, no men were found but, when entering the room, the odour of shaving lotion, and the distinctive aroma of cigar or pipe smoke would be heavy in the area from which the sound had emanated. Some staff reported that in the ladies' lounge there is often a lingering aroma of perfume when no perfumed lady is present, and hadn't been for quite some time.

These are not things that happened long ago, but things that continue to happen to this day. A current staff member vividly recalls an almost unbelievable experience from the recent past. She was in the kitchen cleaning up the dishes after a long night and was alone in the building with her back to the cupboards. Sensing a presence in the room and thinking someone had come back to pick up a forgotten item, she glanced over her shoulder to see who it might be. There was no one there, but as she looked a plate rose off the shelf, hovered momentarily, and then, flew at high speed directly at her. Fortunately, it did not hit her, but shattered on the floor at her feet. She says she didn't stay around long after that happened, but it did not dissuade her from returning to her job the next day, as she has for many days since the event. She's intrigued by the idea that some of the many gentleman who have called the club their second home may still be upset that today, it is as valued by ladies as it is by the gentlemen of the community and she'd like to meet one of those men face to face to explain that without the ladies, the club would simply not exist in modern times. That, explanation, she thinks, would clear up all the problems with so called "ghosts of the Union Club."

The Union Club all decked out for a round of Christmas socials, and in keeping with the season, once known for being the best time of year to share ghost tales, perhaps there were some lurking in the basement getting ready to torment the staff at cleaning up time.

Chapter 20

Where Do Ghosts Go When They Go?

Where Do Ghosts Go When They Go?

Well, if you have read this far, you have a pretty good idea of the ghosts that have been encountered over the decades in Saint John. I am sure you have found some of the stories very believable, while others may not have been nearly as convincing.

This is by no means all the ghosts....there's Partridge Island ghosts, church ghosts in Millidgeville, and the ghost of Maggie Vail way out on the Old Black River road, where she and her daughter were murdered by her lover in 1868. Most schools in the area seem to have a janitor ghost, according to students I've shared these tales with. There are red coated soldier ghosts seen in some graveyards, even stories of ghosts of horses and dogs here and there in the city.

In some of the stories, the place where the ghosts were spotted no longer exists, so that begs the question, "Where do ghosts go when they go?"

This then will constitute the last chapter of this collection.

For a few years, all too few, I had the pleasure of working with songstress, storyteller, author, and radio personality, Frances Helyar while presenting Walks n' Talks.

One night, a fog was blowing in off the Bay Shore and obliterating the cement radar addition atop Saint John's Martello Tower as Frances Helyar gathered a group of walkers for a tour of the area once known as Beaconsfield. The walk was called "Fog, Facts, Phantoms and Fantasy on Beaconsfield Heights," and one of the questions Frances hoped to address was, "Where do ghosts go when they go?"

Though she didn't know it, she was about to meet a new ghost, As she spoke to her group, she heard a gasp from among the crowd, and turning, saw a ragged seafarer emerge from the mist of the Tower Hill graveyard and cross Whipple Street to her position in the Martello Tower parking lot.

"You should have seen the looks on the faces of the cruise ship tourists visiting the tower who had no idea we were about to start a ghost walk," Frances told me later.

The image they saw was that of Daniel Keymore, the ghost of West Saint John, who I was impersonating that night, and whose story you now know if you did not skip Chapter 2.

Frances was about to address the question that has stumped many of us, and that is, "Where do ghosts go when they go?"

Not only is Saint John Harbour's Navy Island home of Keymore gone, but there are at least half a dozen other ghosts in the vicinity of Martello Tower all of whom no longer have homes to haunt. These include a red coated soldier whose barracks are gone, a hermit whose house was burned, and a sailor who haunted the old potato shed that has, sadly, slipped into the harbour, and a land baron, whose palatial house at Tilton's Corner was converted to a hospital, and then torn down in the mid 90's.

So, after explaining a bit of the background of the 1812 Martello Tower on the Parks Canada sponsored tour, Frances broke into song, as she was wont to do, asking?

> "Where do ghosts go when they go?
> Where do they hide, I want to know,
> When their haunts are all torn down,
> Where can these spooky spooks be found?"

She was referring to the best known ghost of the area, the Jewett Castle ghost who once lived in a mansion at the corner of Lancaster Avenue and Prince Street. The location was known for years as Tilton's Corner in honour of the first family to live there.

She was not the first to question what happens to ghosts when the house they haunt is no more.

In fact, when the Castle was torn down in 1951, the "Saint John Evening Times Globe" addressed the question in a headline that read:

"Will Ghost of Castle still walk, is question. Shadowy figure said to frequent Jewett Home."

The paper went on to ask, "This is the question haunting persons interested in the historic old wooden building soon to be demolished in the $1,200,000 construction of the Lancaster Hospital."

The story continued, "To (some) it may come as a surprise to learn that the hospital has had a ghost. The wraith is mentioned in a history of Lancaster Hospital, from 1869 to 1947, written by Marjorie G. Staples and S. Scott MacCorkell." They wrote:

"No history of the hospital would be complete without mentioning the ghost, said to be the 'Shade of Jewett,' which seems to claim the top floor of the original building for its own. Here lights go on in unoccupied rooms, closed doors open, and at times a shadowy figure swathed in a long gray coat is said to have been seen walking up the stairs."

The story noted Jewett's Castle was built in 1869 by Edward D. Jewett for his bride, and located at a site overlooking the Reversing Falls at the mouth of the St. John River. The house originally stood amid four acres of lawns and gardens on a solid granite basement with a massive granite stairway that led up to the front entrance which was located in the centre of an ornate tower. Inside, there was fancy woodwork, frescoes on the walls, a marble fireplace and crystal chandeliers. Nothing but the best for Jewett, who without doubt was the most successful of West Side lumber barons.

After the death of Mr. Jewett, the property was sold in 1884 to the Union Baptist Educational Society for use as a seminary and then in 1907 was bought by J. Harvey Brown to be used as a school for deaf children. It continued as the Deaf and Dumb Institute until 1918 when it was bought by the Dominion Government and became the Lancaster Military Hospital.

By the time the 1951 upgrading had started, it was widely believed that the Jewett ghost roamed the hospital freely and that there was at least one room the ghost preferred which had to be left unoccupied.

When the hospital was torn down after serving as accommodations for the 1985 Canada Games, the question to be asked was, and still is, "Where did the Shade of Jewett go?"

Or as Frances sang it right on the site of the old hospital:

"Where do ghosts go when they go?
Where do they hide, I want to know,
When their haunts are all torn down,

Where can these spooky spooks be found?"

Frances did not get an answer that night, but a few days later, Frank Etwell called me to say he knew where the ghost hung out. "It's just down the street, at an inn," he claimed, adding, "I'll be getting a photo for you to prove it. Two friends were in there and had their photo taken in the doorway and right between them, well, there's this ghost. You'll see."

Soon after this incident, Frank moved to Ontario and I guess he's forgotten all about the "Shade of Jewett" as I have never received the photo from him. Frances also moved to Ontario, but comes back to Saint John occasionally, and when she does, she still asks me the same old question, "Where do ghosts go when they go Dave?" I still don't have an answer for her, but I'll keep trying!

And I hope, having read these tales, you will keep your eye out for ghosts, either those who have moved, or those who hang around places you wish they would leave.

Let me leave you with a couple final thoughts, though. If you encounter a ghost, simply ask the ghost what it wants you to do for it. If it has an uncompleted task, you might be able to help, and not only will you have a story to share, but over the years, wills have been located, money that was hidden away found, jewellery recovered. Finally, think of this. In collecting more than 250 stories province wide, there is not one of them where there was a mean spirited ghost out to do harm. That's a good thought to conclude with.

Frances Helyar at Martello Tower where she was about to ask, "Where do ghosts go when they go?"

The Ghost of John usually does his story-telling at New River Beach, but has been known to come to Saint John on occassion in his quest to find someone to bury him with his buddies who died in the Saxby Gale of October 4, 1869.

Other Books on Saint John Topics

by David Goss

- Saint John West and its Neighbours with Fred Miller- Arcadia 1995
- 150 Years of Caring- The continuing history of Canada' Oldest Mental Health Facility- Mindcare- 1998
- Saint John West Volume 11 with Fred Miller- Arcadia 1999
- Brightening the Corner Where You Are- The story of Saint John Energy- Impresses 2002
- West Side Stories- Nimbus 2004
- Saint John Curiosities- Nimbus 2008
- Saint John 1877-1980- Arcadia 2009
- East Saint John with Harold Wright- Arcadia 2011
- Historic Saint John Street with Harold Wright- Nimbus 2013

On New Brunswick Topics with Some Saint John Content

- Old Tyme Christmas in New Brunswick- Arcadia 1997
- Tall Tales and Curious Happenings- Nimbus 2002
- St George and Its Neighbours with Elizabeth Toy- Arcadia 2002
- It Happened in New Brunswick- Nimbus 2007
- Only in New Brunswick- Nimbus 2011